How to be a Brilliant English Teacher

How to be a Brilliant English Teacher addresses many of the anxieties that English teachers face in the classroom and offers focused and realistic solutions. Packed with practical advice drawn from the author's extensive experience, it will transform your teaching.

The book is anecdotal and readable, and teachers can dip into it for innovative lesson ideas or read it from cover to cover as a short, enjoyable course which uncovers exciting teaching practices and principles. Aspects of teaching English covered include:

- starting with Shakespeare
- studying poetry
- learning to plan
- living with objectives
- managing behaviour
- big and small texts
- drama
- differentiation
- evaluating your work

Both trainee and practising English teachers will find the practical advice and wealth of ideas in this book will improve their skills, enhance their teaching and be of great support.

Trevor Wright is currently in charge of English secondary teacher education at University College Worcester. He has over thirty years of teaching experience.

Mandie Wright wrote the chapter on Drama. She works with the Royal Shakespeare Company, New York University, and University College Worcester.

How to be a Brilliant English Teacher

Trevor Wright

Routledge
Taylor & Francis Group

LONDON AND NEW YORK

First published 2005 by Routledge
2 Park Square, Milton Park, Abingdon, Oxon OX14 4RN

Simultaneously published in the USA and Canada
by Taylor & Francis Inc
270 Madison Ave, New York, NY 10016

Reprinted 2006

Routledge is an imprint of the Taylor & Francis Group, an informa business

© 2005 Trevor Wright and Mandie Wright for Chapter 9

Typeset in Sabon and GillSans by Keystroke, Jacaranda Lodge, Wolverhampton
Printed and bound in Great Britain by MPG Books Ltd, Bodmin

Every effort has been made to ensure that the advice and information in
this book is true and accurate at the time of going to press. However,
neither the publisher nor the authors can accept any legal responsibility
or liability for any errors or omissions that may be made. In the case of
drug administration, any medical procedure or the use of technical
equipment mentioned within this book, you are strongly advised to
consult the manufacturer's guidelines.

British Library Cataloguing in Publication Data
A catalogue record for this book is available from the British Library

Library of Congress Cataloging in Publication Data
A catalog record for this book has been requested

ISBN 10: 0–415–33245–1 (hbk)
ISBN 10: 0–415–33246–X (pbk)

ISBN 13: 978–0–415–33245–3 (hbk)
ISBN 13: 978–0–415–33246–0 (pbk)

Contents

Tables

Acknowledgments

With thanks to Mandie Wright, for Chapter 9, to Shaun Hughes for the illustrations and to Wendy Logan for the index.

A Martian Sends a Postcard Home by Craig Raine is reproduced by permission of David Godwin Associates. *Not My Best Side* and *Horticultural Show* by U. A. Fanthorpe are reproduced by permission of Peterloo Poets. Uccello's painting, *Saint George and the Dragon*, is reproduced by permission of the National Gallery.

Introduction

It's a condition of being an English teacher, whether in training or in post, that you want to be better. There are areas of your practice (perhaps the use of learning objectives, evaluation, differentiation, teaching drama or approaching Shakespeare) where you would like to improve; but it's also a condition of the job that you don't have much if any time for reading theoretical texts. This book, which is rooted in the practice of good English teaching, sets out directly and personally to provide a readable and practical resource based on extensive experience of teaching and training teachers. It moves between example and principle, drawing out fundamentals through specifics and anecdotes. It can be read from start to finish or dipped into for direct, illustrated advice on issues in your own work or training. It's easy to read, occasionally comical, and consistently serious.

How are you actually supposed to differentiate? Are learning objectives restrictive and impossible to think up? Why does everybody hate poetry? Is the apostrophe in fact impossible? Why won't Year 8 actually do anything? How do you prepare pupils for GCSE without the serial murder of Jane Eyre? Answers to such questions centre on a progressive account of teaching principles which have been developed from extensive experience of training teachers, teaching and examining.

This book offers practical and explicit guidance which can create a step-change in the quality of your classroom work, based on straightforward and accessible ideas:

* Good learning and good behaviour management are the same thing.
* Classroom success depends on planning rather than charisma.

- Preparation is the most important thing a teacher does.
- Learning objectives make life easier, not harder.
- Literary reverence is counter-productive.
- The *poetry voice* has turned generations of children against poetry.
- *Background* is wonderful but it belongs in the background.
- The study of texts starts with confident reader reaction, not technical analysis.
- Comparison is necessary, easy and criminally neglected.
- Drama isn't about doing little plays.
- Evaluation is the beginning, not the end, of the learning process.

Two or three years ago, one of my sixth-formers wrote in a leaving card, *Thank you for making English the one lesson that nobody ever wanted to miss.* Teaching isn't a popularity contest, but I was especially touched by this, because I normally imagine sixth-formers sitting in rows in the common-room thinking up ingenious reasons for not going to lessons. This book sets out to guide teachers from being competent or good to being brilliant and each chapter offers examples and route maps for that simple journey.

Chapter 1

Shakespeare
First contact

It's an agreed national ethic that we don't like Shakespeare. In general knowledge quizzes, the Shakespeare question is left until last and finally approached with a sheepish grin; knowing nothing about Shakespeare is something to be proud of. Children who have never read or seen him groan at the mention of his name. In this respect, Shakespeare is the maths of English. He is also the only compulsory author in the English National Curriculum.

How have we allowed this to happen? Perhaps the first time you saw Shakespeare it was in an elderly, soft-covered book. Somebody had written *I have never been so Bord (sic) in all my life* across the cast list, which contained such promising names as Titania (Queen of the fairies, apparently) and Puck. The teacher handed out the parts to some keen volunteers who read clearly and entirely without understanding for the next six weeks.

First contact with Shakespeare is a highly significant moment for children and deserves some careful planning on your part. This is generally true of openings: schemes of work and individual lessons often live or die in the first few moments.

Transforming your teaching of Shakespeare is easy, and is an object lesson in transforming your teaching in general. Like all teaching successes, it primarily requires thoughtful and focused planning, based on the gifts of the material and its connections with the children. When considering pupils' first contact with Shakespeare, there are things you can and should do, and there are things you shouldn't, and in examining them, we will arrive at some preliminary principles about being a brilliant English teacher.

Don't show the video first

Of course we want children to see Shakespeare; reading a play anywhere, and especially in a classroom, is an unnatural act, and much work has been done, especially by Rex Gibson, on how to bring Shakespeare to life. But starting with the video is a fatal error.

This isn't only because there are more bad Shakespeare videos than good ones, or because even good ones are still difficult for people new to Shakespeare, but because the biggest ally you have when teaching a text is the story. Children don't want to spend weeks ploughing through a story when they already know how it ends. This is like watching a taped football match when you already know the final score.

Don't choose a play because you love it

It's a significant principle that you choose teaching material for the pupils, not for yourself. You may have loved *Twelfth Night* at school, but then you were good at English, and this is a handicap for you now in a number of ways that we will look at later.

For example, many teachers choose a comedy, because adolescents like a good laugh. It's an understandable decision. But comedy scripts are quite often not funny when read in a classroom. In the case of Shakespeare, the jokes usually have to be analysed. For example, in *Twelfth Night*, the comic character Feste constantly says things like "Bonos dies, Sir Toby; for as the old hermit of Prague that never saw pen and ink very wittily said to a niece of King Gorboduc: that is, is." Any joke that has to be explained has already failed. If this is your hilarious secret weapon in selling Shakespeare to Year 9, you're in trouble.

Many teachers choose *Romeo and Juliet* because it's about adolescent love and because a few years ago there was a massively popular film and these are good instincts; but be careful. One thing that children new to Shakespeare will often say is "Why doesn't he just say what he means?" The teacher needs to be able to explain that Shakespeare doesn't use complex expression (as they see it) just to show off, or to be difficult. For example, a thirteen-year-old coming to this speech of Mercutio's:

> O, then I see Queen Mab hath been with you.
> She is the fairies' midwife, and she comes
> In shape no bigger than an agate stone
> On the forefinger of an alderman
> Drawn with a team of little atomies
> Over men's noses as they lie asleep –

is likely to have his worst fears about Shakespeare confirmed.

Don't start with background

A lively understanding of context will enrich any study, but in the stage of "first contact" you must above all else be making connections between the pupils and the material. Many children come to Shakespeare with the received attitude that he's alien, ancient and difficult. In fact he deals with murder, seduction, incest, prostitution, comedy, war, betrayal, disguise, deception, ambition, sex, cannibalism, jealousy, violence and the supernatural, but nevertheless children know by cultural osmosis that he's boring. Doing pictures of the Globe Theatre or knowing that Juliet, as well as being four hundred years old, was also a boy in tights will only serve to reinforce the perceived distance and alienness of the text.

Make the connection

I used to work through the plays, with children reading, explaining bits and trying to make it interesting as I went along. They weren't bad lessons, though I imagine most of the children were quietly bored most of the time. When I started planning with the clear focus of connecting children to the text, my lessons changed dramatically.

Here is an extended example of first contact, in this case between a Year 9 class and *A Midsummer Night's Dream*, a very popular play. I've set this out in some detail because we can find a number of generic principles and practices which can be adapted for other texts – for example, for the Key Stage 3 texts. Although the *Dream* is a comedy, and frequently chosen for the (in my view highly questionable) reason that children like fairies, I have chosen to focus on non-comedic and non-fairy issues in the play's opening.

A group of nobles from Athens appears and discusses getting married, or "nuptials". After some time, more characters arrive and a family dispute is presented to the Duke. In terms of first contact with Shakespeare, this is all quite unpromising. There are fairies in the cast list, which don't generally impress adolescents; people's names are unpronounceable or, in a few cases, potentially obscene; and of course the language presents serious difficulties. A simple statement like "our nuptial hour draws on apace" is probably meaningless to most of the children, and this is only the first line of the play.

It is a simple matter to make this first contact something the children will enjoy, remember when they go home, and want to get on with next time. You just have to consider what the point of connection is between the pupils and the text. A girl wants to marry a boy, but her father objects. In fact he prefers another boy. This is in no sense uninteresting to most fourteen-year-olds. Many of them live with this kind of unwanted parental interference on a daily basis. They have opinions about it.

So you have decided on your point of contact, which will highlight issues with which pupils can identify, and about which they will have opinions. Opinions are a major weapon in the brilliant teacher's armoury. Adolescents contain large numbers of opinions, and allowing them into your lessons will generate energy and involvement. Pupils are more interested in judging Hermia's father than in understanding him, and this is the legitimate business of an audience, anyway. So now you just have to construct a lesson that focuses on issues, attitudes and opinions around Hermia's predicament. From now on the planning is easy. You simply have to provide a structure that focuses where you want to focus. This structure will involve pupil and teacher activity and the editing of the text in order to manage pupils' first contact with it.

Having made this straightforward planning decision, I sat down and made a simple lesson activity. It took me about twenty minutes. What is set out below is a pupils' activity sheet. They worked on this in pairs. They had no idea that it was connected with Shakespeare; they had not at that point been given the books. The activity is self-contained; you can answer the questions using only the information on the sheet, never having read the play. Try it yourself now.

Table 1.1 There is a problem . . .

Theseus is the Duke
Egeus is Hermia's father
Hermia loves Lysander
Demetrius and Lysander both love Hermia

A   This man hath my consent to marry her . . .

B   I would my father look'd but with my eyes!

C   . . . Or else the law of Athens yields you up,
     Which by no means we may extenuate,
     To death, or to vow a single life.

D   This man hath bewitched the bosom of my child . . .

E   But I beseech your Grace, that I may know
     The worst that may befall me in this case,
     If I refuse..?

F   You have her father's love, Demetrius;
     Let me have Hermia's; do you marry him!

	Who says?	To/about whom?	Meaning?	Attitude?
A				
B				
C				
D				
E				
F				

This is the central activity, and its objective is to support pupils in understanding a situation and its related attitudes. It succeeds on three levels:

It edits the text

In fact, as editing goes, this is fairly drastic! But, in general, editing Shakespeare is a good thing. You have never seen a production or read a text that wasn't edited; Shakespeare can stand editing; reverence isn't a practical attitude, and Shakespeare is a practical writer. The editing here points at the central focus, obviously; it also presents children with their first contact in the form of tiny, manageable bits of text set into the context of a structured activity. Even so, the text isn't easy for them; I love Lysander's joke in F, and I want them to see the comedy there ("I'll marry the daughter, you can marry the father, he seems quite keen on you!") because it's modern, accessible, sarcastic humour, but just the grammatical inversion of *do you marry him* will make children read it as a question and lose the point. In fact I added the exclamation mark myself to try to avoid this.

It's structured

As well as being focused on a particular aspect of the text, the activity is structured. The provision of a simple table to complete is powerfully focusing: it generates purpose and concentration.

It's oral pair work

We need especially here to build confidence, and working in pairs enables pupils to explore and try out different interpretations in an oral arena where things don't become crystallised too early and where they don't feel too exposed.

This pair discussion builds to a whole-class version of the family argument and possible solutions to it. But in itself it is not the full picture. As an activity it still needs to be set into the context of the pupils' experiences. They need to see this family dispute in the context of others.

The personal context

The lesson (and in fact the whole study of the *Dream*) began with a discussion of family rows. We will talk elsewhere about the openings of lessons, but a sound principle is always to begin concrete – don't begin abstract. Asking "What do families argue about?" as your opening salvo might work, but it's a big question, and might simply provoke an uneasy silence as the pupils try to understand what kind of answer you might want. Awkward silences like that at lesson beginnings must be avoided at all costs. They are painfully hard to recover from. There are two tricks to ensure that this doesn't happen: ask a concrete question ("What was the last family row in your house about?"); and invite two minutes' jotting before the discussion, so everyone has something to say.

This builds into a whole-class discussion about typical causes of family arguments, and the teacher makes a list of pupil suggestions on the board – bedrooms, food, curfews, and, inevitably, boyfriends and girlfriends. Some anecdotes are exchanged. Some discussion of fair and unfair sanctions is included. This could all take twenty minutes, and is then followed by the *There is a problem . . .* sheet.

It's quite possible that transitions between activities are the most important learning moments in your lesson. When children make the connections themselves, it's especially rewarding and strongly indicative that the lesson is going well. In this lesson pupils will often say, as they do the structured activity, "This is like what we were talking about earlier." After the activity, you move on to the text itself, and again they will often see the links for themselves. What you have done is present two layers of warm-up, the first associating the text with their own experiences and so providing confidence as well as engagement, and the second moving everyday themes closer to Shakespeare's language. Now it's time to read the text.

People worry about reading Shakespeare, especially when approaching (say) a mixed-ability Year 9 with their SAT play. It helps to remember that Shakespeare is the archetypal mixed-ability author. All teachers know that everyone went to Shakespeare's theatre; in fact, the most expensive seat at the Globe cost thirty times as much as the cheapest. Virtually every social class and every level of education enjoyed Shakespeare. We often tell children about this, but rarely seem to recognise its significance for us as teachers. He is ultimately differentiated, and this has powerful implications for the plotting, structure and language of the plays, which we can use in our planning and teaching.

One implication of this is that the speeches themselves often differentiate. Within the imagery and complexity there are frequently blunt, summary statements and these support and give confidence to children. In *Lear*, Edmund speaks a long, introductory soliloquy which is almost deliberately complicated; but, after fifteen lines of bombastic rhetoric, he says, "Edgar, I must have your land." Five

monosyllables sum up his intentions with absolute, direct simplicity. Henry V uses similarly simple language to summarise the burden of kingship – "We must bear all" – within a long and rich soliloquy. Theseus describes one of Hermia's options as concerning abjuring the society of men, mew'd for aye in a shady cloister, being a barren sister; but he also helpfully explains that he's talking about her becoming a *nun*. The explanation is there, and children must become used to working outwards from the bits of text they understand, rather than staring disconsolately at the bits they don't. And an acknowledgement that straightforwardness is often to be found is another reason for not simply working line-by-line. Indeed, translation has no part to play in the study of Shakespeare.

Another aspect of Shakespearian differentiation is that there is much variety of shaping on the stage. Two-handed scenes are followed by crowds, then by soliloquies, for example, and this should make class reading a flexible and dynamic activity. Dishing out the parts and then waiting while the children struggle on, stopping at the ends of most lines, manfully reading out the stage directions, thinking of other things while they wait their turn and then missing it when it finally comes – do you remember your own impatience at school with this process? It doesn't take long to plan the reading, using the text shapes to guide you, and bearing in mind your overall objectives of building confidence and connections with the text.

For example, at the opening of the *Dream*, Theseus and Hippolyta talk about their marriage. This has nothing to do with your chosen focus, so leave it out (you can always come back to it later if you must). Egeus then appears and makes quite a long speech about the family dispute, and this introduces your chosen focus area, so the pupils must understand it. It's a single-handed speech, not really a dialogue: you should read this yourself.

There is research to suggest that children are likely to be embarrassed by teachers trying too hard with the reading. I personally love to read the part of Lear (it's increasingly enjoyable to me as I get older); but we must avoid the reverential hush, the attempted grandeur, the poetry voice. The poetry voice is on its own responsible for turning generations of children against poetry. Poetry is just efficient language. So read the Egeus speech for meaning; in fact, you read it for the particular meaning you need. It's expository: it introduces key characters and the initial plot situation; it couldn't be more helpful.

Much excellent work has been done about active Shakespeare teaching but this doesn't always finally address the text itself. I have stood in the corner of many drama studios where children have been attempting lively activities whose effects have been limited by the fact that, ultimately, there were still words and phrases there that they didn't understand. You can physicalise the text yourself, in the classroom, in a non-threatening way. Just having a pupil stand up to represent each named character, so the class can see the triangle as you read, will help them to visualise the text. Plan your reading – so many teachers read text clearly but without a clear focus on their own requirements. Egeus says:

> Full of vexation come I, with complaint
> Against my <u>child, my daughter Hermia.</u>
> Stand forth, <u>Demetrius</u>. My noble lord,
> <u>This</u> man hath my <u>consent</u> to marry her.
> Stand forth, <u>Lysander</u>: and my gracious duke,
> <u>This</u> man hath <u>bewitch'd</u> the bosom of my child;
> Thou, thou, Lysander, thou hast given her rhymes,
> And interchanged love-tokens with my child:
> Thou hast by moonlight at her window sung,
> With <u>feigning</u> voice verses of <u>feigning</u> love,
> And stolen the impression of her fantasy
> With <u>bracelets of thy hair, rings, gawds, conceits,</u>
> <u>Knacks, trifles, nosegays, sweetmeats,</u> messengers
> Of strong prevailment in unharden'd youth:
> With cunning hast thou <u>filch'd</u> my daughter's heart,
> Turn'd her obedience, which is due to me,
> To stubborn harshness.

Try, for example, simply underlining and then emphasising all references to the characters and relationships, which are being introduced to the audience for the first time. So, stress "child", "daughter", "Hermia", "Demetrius" as you read. But also stress "this" in the phrase "<u>this</u> man", pointing at the pupil who stands (he doesn't have to act or speak) for Demetrius or Lysander. The stressing of "this", unlikely though it sounds, transforms the reading and understanding of this speech, because it conforms to your need to physically set out the agenda. You, Shakespeare and Egeus are all doing the same thing here – explaining what's going on to people who don't yet know (the nobles, the audience, the class). Shakespeare is your ally: use the

synergy by recognising the expository function of the speech. It is
written to do exactly what you as a teacher need it to do.

You need to be reading this yourself because it's early, it's
extended and it's essential. Even your best reader (who has had no
preparation) can't be expected to emphasise the key points. Your
emphasis needs to be stronger than you might imagine. For example,
you need to show the antithesis between your fondness for one
man and your disgust for the other. A simple opposition like this is
memorable for children. You don't have to be a great actor or even
especially histrionic to do this, but you do have to think about your
reading. I have heard this read many times by teachers who emphasise, for example, the romantic nature of *bracelets* and *nosegays*
rather than the sarcastic fury that really lies behind these details.

At the end of this speech, Egeus, having set out the dispute, asks
for judgment. At this point you should stop reading the text and
immediately discuss with the class what will and should happen next.
This allows two powerful classroom allies of the brilliant teacher
– prediction and opinion – to generate energy and engagement.
Prediction forces analysis and imaginative involvement. It also
provides a comparative momentum for the text to come – was I right,
or will something unexpected happen? It can be used with any
fictional or non-fictional text (and is another reason for not showing
the video first). Opinion, as we've already seen, attaches pupils to
texts, especially if, through warm-ups, you have created a discursive
environment around the text's themes. Children will be furious that
Hermia's only options seem to be to do as she's told or die. They will
want to discuss (probably in pairs) other solutions. They are already
learning a good deal about theatre – that it's open to interpretation,
that different audiences can have different opinions, that an audience
operates by assimilation and prediction as it watches.

They aren't learning about blank verse, about imagery. This
chapter is called *First contact* and this kind of linguistic analysis isn't
appropriate in the early stages. Later it will become fascinating (we
hope) to many of your children, but the brilliant teacher learns to
focus on appropriate learning issues, not to try to cover everything.

Egeus' appeal for judgment is followed by a two-handed section
where Theseus talks to Hermia. This is an opportunity for the pupils
to read the text in pairs, following Shakespeare's shaping. Pair
reading is the next logical step after listening to the teacher read: they
now have the text in their mouths, and they can try it out in a non-
threatening environment. They will also begin to recognise bits of

text from the earlier activity, and this will give them confidence. However, the brilliant teacher remembers that children usually benefit from a focus for reading and/or listening. Ask the key question *before* the reading, so they can look out for it. Here, try asking them to read in pairs and then discuss what Hermia's three options are. A whole-class discussion of these options will follow, blending comprehension with opinion – what are her options now? Are they reasonable? Which would you choose? What do you think she'll do? In answer to that last question, a number of children regularly guess that she'll run away from home; and that's what she does.

In fact, the *Which would you choose?* question provokes fascinating debate. The answer is by no means obvious. Simply ranking the three alternatives in order of preference – singly, then in pairs, then as a class – causes heated arguments. You can marry someone you don't love; or become a nun or monk (and therefore marry nobody); or die. You may be surprised by the range of preferences in the room.

I have set out this lesson in some detail because it introduces some of the themes of this guide to being a better English teacher. These include:

- Planning from the pupils' point of view
- Having absolutely clear focus
- Connecting the material to the pupils
- Learning through activities
- The importance of structure
- Clear and identifiable progression
- The centrality of transitions
- Taking the benefits of the text into your teaching
- The value of opinions
- The value of predictions
- The significance of warm-up
- Not trying to cover everything
- Variety of classroom groupings
- The particular usefulness of pair work
- The significance of good teacher-reading
- The value of focus before reading.

If you have followed the description of the *Dream* activity then you already have an understanding of these issues, and this is a pretty good starting agenda for becoming a brilliant English teacher.

Approaches

We've made the simple point that starting Shakespeare requires structure, focus and a point of contact. The *Dream* offers the family dispute, and parental interference in adolescents' business. When starting *Macbeth*, you may find that your pupils are besotted by witches, just as they may be enchanted by fairies in the *Dream*, but in my experience it's unlikely. *Macbeth* offers many better initial contact points – for example, the repercussions of one evil action, the subsequent line-up of lying, further deceptions, more murders – this pattern is familiar to many teenagers (not literally including the murders, of course). The predictions are fascinating not because of their supernatural origins (twenty-first-century adolescents think that witches are stupid) but because of their influence on Macbeth's actions – do horoscopes actually modify our behaviour? And the problem-solving is absorbing – how can a forest move? How can a man not be born of a woman? Predictions are a powerful way of involving pupils in texts, and *Macbeth* is made for predictions. *Richard III* features similar themes of power and ambition but also offers a central character who is adept at manipulation, seduction and bullying – persuasive tactics which adolescents encounter often. There's also the discussion of whether we like Richard – like Iago, he has many asides and soliloquies, and can be played very attractively. Are villains more attractive than heroes? What makes a good leader? At the end of the play both Richard and his opponent Henry make persuasive speeches to their armies. A good starting-point would be to consider the differences, for example in vocabulary. Henry's speech includes words like *Loving countrymen . . . prayers . . . saints . . . wives . . . children . . . God . . . share . . . justice*; while Richard favours *cowards . . . Pell-mell . . . Hell . . . vagabonds . . . rascals . . . vomit . . . whip . . . lash . . . rats* and *bastard*. Which language is the more persuasive? *Much Ado* features match-making among friends who deceive Beatrice and Benedick to bring them together – a plot direct from teenage soap-opera, and an excellent place to start. *The Tempest* deals with a father/daughter (so parent/child) relationship within the wider theme of freedom and control – again, themes very close to adolescent experience, and so significant places to begin planning first contact. It only takes a few minutes of planning to liberate the text from class reading and to attach it to the lives of your audience – which is surely what any playwright would want to happen, as well as what a brilliant teacher needs to do.

Chapter 2

Planning
The third element

I could never understand chemistry at school, despite my teachers' efforts, and I have quite clear memories of trying very hard to believe that there were tiny particles revolving at breakneck speed within the solid desk I was leaning on. We all tried, but I couldn't get it, and that was about the most useful experience of all for me as a teacher.

The problem is that you were good at English when you went to school. It is of course essential that you should know a lot about your subject, but when planning work it's even more important to recognise that the pupils won't know what you're talking about. There are three elements in the learning transaction – you, the material and the pupils. This is obvious, but I have many times looked at planning and teaching which were based entirely on the first two.

Your progression as a teacher will be marked by your increasing concern for pupil reaction and understanding in your planning. You will move from teaching to learning.

Your knowledge of what the pupils already know will vary greatly. There are many formal and informal sources of information and of course you will be basing the content of your teaching on a progressive view of what they've already learnt from you and other people. The fact remains, however, that you are almost bound to be teaching them things they don't already know. It would be odd if you weren't.

Planning is the most important thing that a teacher does. More than classroom presence or charismatic delivery, planning ensures trust, security, good behaviour and progressive learning. Problems which may seem to have nothing to do with it, such as behaviour management problems, are most often solved by better planning. And while planning, you should consistently evaluate what you're proposing from the viewpoint of someone for whom your ideas, instructions and materials are completely new. This requires an imaginative dimension to lesson planning, but English teachers are good at imagination. Good teachers understand knowledge, but brilliant teachers understand ignorance. Remember and savour your chemistry moment.

In fact, all plans (wedding plans, career plans, holiday plans) are essentially acts of imagination. You are projecting what should and what might happen; you are guessing at the possible reactions to and repercussions of your decisions. You are anticipating good and bad outcomes. Lesson plans are no different, and they only become alive and effective when you recognise their fundamentally imaginative nature.

This may sound whimsical but it has systematic, concrete implications for the efficiency of your teaching. It means first and foremost that you are creating events and experiences for pupils, not broadcasting information to them, and at every planning stage you should be imagining their possible reactions, associations and confusions. So your lesson plans need to distinguish between teacher and pupil activity. You need to consider their access routes to the learning, not just the content of it.

One of the best lessons I have ever seen was a Year 8 maths lesson. The teacher entered the classroom and drew a vertical line down the middle of the whiteboard. He then drew a small cross to one side of the line. The children watched him as he paused; then he drew another identical cross opposite the first, on the other side of the line.

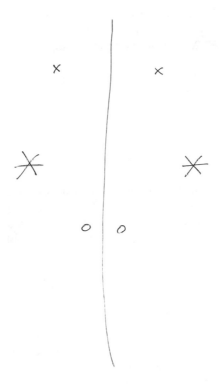

After another pause, he drew another cross, somewhere above the original cross, and offered the board marker to the class. A few hands went up. A volunteer took the marker and drew the fourth cross, exactly opposite the third one. And so the lesson went on for some minutes, the children increasingly active. Not a word was spoken.

Although a maths lesson, and a very elegant piece of teaching, this was also a lesson in literacy. It was about symmetry, of course. It worked almost perfectly for a number of reasons. It had a single, clear and focused objective; it was highly interactive; it generated the need for a piece of learning and then met that need.

Let's consider that last point. The teacher could have come in and said, "Today we're going to talk about symmetry." (He writes the word on the board). "OK. Symmetry What's symmetry? Does anyone know? No? Well . . ." And he proceeds to define and illustrate the word.

You've sat in that lesson dozens of times. I've taught it dozens of times. "Today we're going to talk about metaphors. What's a metaphor . . . ?" When you start considering the third element in the planning chain – the pupils – you start to see what an imperfect approach this is. The questions are irritating. I don't know what a metaphor is, no. If I did, you wouldn't need to be teaching it to me, would you? So why are you asking me? Don't you know? Don't you know what I know? Let's get on with it. Just tell me about the flaming metaphors.

If you begin your lesson with the word, the concept, the key learning, you can only travel backwards. The lesson becomes a retrospective definition. Instead, plan your lesson to move forward towards the key learning moments. After six or eight minutes drawing crosses and then circles in varying positions and colours, the maths teacher started a discussion about the children's decisions. They explained to him, using words like *opposite, mirror, same place*. They reached a point where, in order to continue the conversation, they needed an appropriate word. The teacher, having created the concept, having explored it through activity, having generated the need for the word, finally supplied it. The pupils, rather than being bored, mildly interested, passive, were actively grateful. They were relieved, because they needed the word, and now they had it. When they went home that night, they would be able to tell anyone who asked them what symmetry was.

We learn when there's a need to learn. We don't learn just by being told. We don't learn words from dictionaries. After watching the symmetry lesson, I devised a lesson based on similes. I was in fact teaching Charles Causley's poem *Timothy Winters* to Year 7.

I draw on the whiteboard a large egg shape and I write the label *head like an egg* with an arrow to it. This is cartoon scrawl, not elegance. I then add a feature – for example, I draw a large, red eye and write *eye like a tomato*. One by one the pupils come to the board and add features (*ear like a biro, spots like baked beans*). This is a comical lesson, and every child can have a go.

After this, of course, we discuss the character we've created. He isn't beautiful. He certainly isn't symmetrical. We might name him. We might write a class poem about him. What we certainly do is reach the moment of discussion of what we've done when the pupils need the word *simile*. We then spend time on the word, including on its spelling (since only six people in England can spell *simile*). We define it together, and this includes understanding why you might use it.

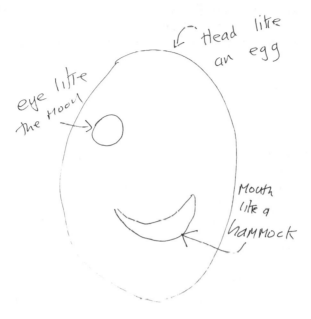

There is of course no point at all in teaching children what a simile is if they don't have some sense of its effect on them as readers. Why is *spots like baked beans* better than just *spots*? Here we have spent twenty minutes laughing and thinking up increasingly outrageous (and occasionally obscene) similes. We now *know* from our experience that similes liven things up; they can, we now know, make things funnier. We have discovered this in creating them. We haven't just been told it; we know it. Next we read a poem – in this case, *Timothy Winters* – which features similes (*ears like bombs, teeth like splinters*) and we can recognise and talk about the effects of those similes because similes and their effects are already ours.

All planning comes from learning objectives, as we will be discussing later (in Chapter 3). This wasn't a difficult lesson to devise, once I'd decided that enjoying similes was my objective. It's a myth that lively lessons like this take hours of resource preparation. All this needed was one idea and a board marker. A consideration of the differences between this lesson and the "OK, everyone, who knows what a simile is?" approach will take your teaching up several notches.

One key issue in this planning is the association of creative and analytical work. So many children will come to similes for the first time when the teacher points one out in a text. A good teacher will take time at a moment like this to discuss the effects of the simile on the reader, rather than just defining the term and moving on. A very good teacher will pause long enough to allow the pupils to try and write some similes of their own. A brilliant teacher will have already decided that similes is a key lesson objective and will place the creative work first, as in the lesson described above.

It is almost always right to use creative approaches alongside analytical ones. You don't learn to drive by watching somebody driving. Creative approaches provide experiences rather than information. If you want your pupils to investigate the language of radio news bulletins, it is of course a good idea to analyse bulletins which you've recorded on tape. This is an approach favoured by the *Key Stage 3 Framework for Teaching English* – we could call it text-type analysis, and we will talk about that more in Chapter 7. Children consider the typical language features, the stock vocabulary of the news bulletins. Reporters say, "Over to . . .", they introduce characters in a formulaic way – "Ian, thirty-six, a shop assistant from Marlborough . . ." and so on. Children discover this through analysis. A logical next stage is for them to write their own bulletins, using these language features. This creative dimension consolidates the analysis.

In fact, if you start with the creative activity, asking children to write local radio news bulletins *without* any previous analysis or discussion, you will probably find that they use many of those language features anyway. They already know how news language sounds. The creative approach is often a shortcut to the learning. Children may know much more about language than you think.

Planning backwards

There is nothing more depressing than sitting at a desk with a blank sheet of paper and the prospect of six weeks' teaching stretching before you. What on earth will the first lesson be about? How do I plan for eighteen lessons when I have already taken three hours to come up with nothing much for lesson one?

Stop thinking about lesson one. At all levels (and there are about four levels), all planning starts at the end and works backwards. The *Framework*, which we will examine in Chapter 7, proposes a hierarchy of planning (long-, medium- and short-term planning), which implies the need for planning backwards. You start from knowing what the long-term learning objectives are, and these are interpreted in ever-increasing detail down the hierarchy. So your blank sheet of paper (blank except for the forlorn heading, "Lesson one?") doesn't exist. You begin by knowing what you're going to achieve at the other end.

The medium-term plan exists because you've been given it or you've devised it in terms of long-term objectives. If you follow it, you will be meeting *Framework* and National Curriculum requirements. It is your planning friend. You can see it as a central spine, running through your work. Often, it is centred around a text; your work for those six weeks may be focused on *Skellig*, or *The Merchant of Venice*. Alternatively, it might be based on a set of language objectives – considering persuasive language, for example. Having a central focus for your planning lends consistency and context to the pupils' learning, of course (though beware of death-by-theme, when everyone gets very bored by animals or old age because it's in every single lesson). It also helps you with lesson planning, because the focus generates planning ideas.

Here's an example. In teaching *The Merchant of Venice* to Year 9, you decide to focus on the marriage will. It's good to be selective; don't try to do everything. There are various masque scenes, for example, which just confuse and alienate pupils. It's fine to skip them. You will remember that Portia's dead father left a will whereby she can only marry someone who passes a test, which involves choosing among gold, silver and lead caskets. In fact it's a complex test, involving various inscriptions, rules, images and poems, as well as the caskets. It's necessary to weed out chancers, because Portia is both beautiful and rich. As I write this, I have a beautiful daughter of marriageable age and I think I understand where Portia's dad was coming from. And I'm neither rich nor dead.

This is a terrific plot to follow. As so often with Shakespeare, it's highly differentiated; everyone knows instinctively through fairy-tale logic that the lead casket is the one to pick, but, at a more complex level, there are bewildering rules such as this one: *any man who attempts the test and fails must never marry any other woman*. At first sight, this appears to be an unnecessarily punitive and aggressive rule, and children can't see the point of it. Remember at a moment like this that you must ask them to discuss and justify such rules rather then explaining them yourself.

The best way of gaining an understanding of this rule and the other complexities of Lord Belmont's will is to run a parallel scheme of work where the pupils, working in pairs for the discussion (because it's the discussion that counts, not the product) create their own marriage tests. While they might be reading the various *casket* scenes for certain lessons in the week, at other points in the same week they put the play to one side and work on their own marriage tests. They start by deciding on a list of criteria for the ideal man (or woman). Then they devise the tests – beauty contests, questionnaires, fitness challenges, intelligence tests, reality-TV challenges, interviews, multiple-choice quizzes – to select suitors for their imaginary daughters, or imaginary friends. Finally, they present and explain their tests to each other.

Once again, we are looking at the fusion of creative and analytical work. Working on their own twenty-first-century marriage tests, which on the surface have nothing whatever to do with Shakespeare's characters, they come to understand Shakespeare's text. For example, in their discussions they come to understand that the test needs a mechanism for discouraging opportunists who aren't seriously in love. The serious intentions of candidates need to be proved by their having something to lose and being prepared to lose it; otherwise, anybody could have a go. Agreeing to give up all ideas of marriage to anybody else is one such test.

Here, then, we have in effect two connected spines running for the duration of a medium-term plan – the reading and discussion of a classic text, and the collaborative contemporary language work. Though separate, they will work together to create genuine understanding of a chosen piece of a Shakespeare play. This produces a rational background for short-term planning and lesson planning. Start with the end results and the big picture – not with lesson one.

Planning for variety

The single biggest preoccupation in the National Curriculum is variety and range. You will see that it is referred to several times on every page of the Key Stage 3 and 4 Programme of Study. At an early stage it will help you to consider why this is so.

Of course, children like variety, and it's obvious that pupil boredom doesn't help you in behaviour management, but that isn't why variety is so important. Behind this lies a model of progress, which is a commonsense and accessible model that will help you in your planning.

Progress in your own indigenous language isn't a matter of the linear acquisition of skills. For one thing, development can often seem to go backwards before going forwards – progress is more like a series of loops than a straight line. (For example, spelling can appear to slip backwards when vocabulary is extending; syntax and punctuation can appear to suffer when ideas and sentences are becoming more sophisticated.) And, for another thing, progress isn't along one route, but along increasing numbers of routes. It's helpful to think of progress as *getting better at more things*.

What this means is that the range and repertoire extend. Children get better at understanding and making appropriate language choices across a growing range of language situations. They become better at using formal and informal language, they become explicitly conscious of tone. In Year 7, all letters may look much the same, but in Year 10 pupils know that mums, girlfriends and bank managers all need different handling.

Paramount to all of this is the essential notion of appropriateness to purpose and audience. This above all else is what children must get better at, and they do this by explicit discussion and by being given the widest possible experience of language contexts in their reading, writing, speaking and listening.

So variety isn't a superficial or trivial issue – it's a central one. It's a good idea, therefore, to look at a new medium-term plan and check it for variety. You could consider, for example:

- Is there a balance of reading, writing, speaking and listening?
- Is there a range of fiction and non-fiction reading?
- Is there a range of tone?
- Is there a balance of formal and informal language?
- Is there a balance of standard and non-standard language?
- Is there a balance of modern and not-modern reading?
- Is there reading from other cultures?
- Is there a range of genres?
- Is there a balance of creative and analytical work?
- Is there a range of purposes and audiences?
- Is there a variety of pupil groupings for discussion and collaboration?

You may well not answer "yes" to all of these questions. In many cases, that's fine; you can't cover everything in every scheme of work.

But you should be saying "yes" to a good number of them. For example, if there's no speaking and listening in your medium-term plan, there should be; so you need to adjust it.

Purpose and audience in the real world

Purpose and audience is a recurring phrase in English teaching; it's a phrase that deserves some analysis. Frequently its two components are thought of as one, or as synonymous, so a lesson may offer "Letter to bank manager" as its purpose and audience. If we are to fully exploit the concept, which is capable of considerable subtlety, we need carefully to consider that a given audience does not imply a single purpose. It's the *comparison* between different purposes that counts.

A Year 7 pupil may be asked to write to her mum from Switzerland, where she is on her first school skiing trip. A simple lesson will deal with audience (informal, chatty, affectionate) and purpose (information) at a basic level. But by considering the *range of possible purposes* and how they are likely to affect the writing the teacher moves into a much more challenging area. Why might you write to your mum? You might, for example, want to reassure her, not simply to inform her. Or to persuade her to send more pocket money. Or to persuade her to let you come home straight away. A good teacher will discuss the purpose and audience of this simple activity, but a brilliant one will draw attention to the range of possible purposes and how these might affect the tone and content of the letter. She might make on the whiteboard a collaborative list, based on children's suggestions, of different possible reasons for the letter. She might ask pupils to select from a list of given facts (*we arrived three hours late, the hotel is very nice, the food is peculiar, the café is expensive, my friend fell over and sprained his ankle, the instructor is very good, I'm sharing a room with Debbie who I don't particularly like*, etc.) as would be appropriate to the chosen purpose of the letter.

The effective teacher knows that the purpose of her lesson isn't to get a letter written; it's to understand that a change of purpose changes the letter, and *her lesson activities centre around these changes rather than a single version of the letter itself.* Pupils will readily appreciate that purpose influences their writing (and the writing of others) when they see the possibilities of *two different versions*. The teacher is moving the pupils towards *comparison*, which is extremely powerful and underlines many of the best teaching techniques for appreciating literary and non-literary texts.

Of course one problem is that the real audience for virtually everything is often the teacher, and finding ways of moving beyond this is crucial to sharpening pupils' perceptions. An effective teacher builds real audiences and their real evaluations into her planning. There are audiences available everywhere – in the class, in the school, and beyond, and the brilliant teacher makes use of these routinely, not just for occasional formal presentations. Local newspapers are often very keen to publish; internet sites exist to provide exchange opportunities; public figures may be written to. I once suggested to a Year 8 group that they write to their favourite television and pop stars to find out whether they believed in ghosts. Their first job was to research addresses (record companies, fan clubs, television companies) and then they had to consider ways of making their letters successful. Their *purpose* was simply to elicit a reply from someone who received a lot of fan mail. They discussed in pairs ways of making their letters stand out, considering issues such as courtesy, flattery, sincerity, recipient's personality, humour, and so on. In other words, they had serious, detailed and sustained discussions of tone, audience and purpose, and these discussions were of a quality that would not have been part of a class-bound exercise. (Many replies were received, ranging from signed photographs to quite detailed personal responses to the questions. One famous television magician wrote three closely argued pages about the paranormal. We discussed the replies as part of an evaluation of the letters.)

You are surrounded by real-world texts to analyse and recreate (such as the radio news bulletins we mentioned earlier) and often it's effective to simulate. The *Crime File* is a highly enjoyable medium-term work scheme. Working in pairs, pupils create the story of a crime – probably a murder. They create suspects, red herrings, clues and motives. They then set out to tell the story. However, they tell it with *no narrative at all*; instead, they must assemble the documents surrounding the case. They will make such texts as:

- passports
- police notebook
- sketch maps
- anonymous notes
- driving licences
- ransom notes

- news cuttings
- interview reports
- witness statements
- diary entries
- cheques
- letters
- suicide notes
- credit card vouchers
- court reports
- criminal records

Year 8 pupils will become very preoccupied with the physical appearance of such material, putting documents in the toaster or bleeding over them to make them look authentic; but they will also become interested in the various tones and structures involved in this range of texts, and they will find and look at examples of some of them. There are too many text types here for full text-type analysis (see Chapter 7), but the range and variety is an excellent introduction to the essential concept that texts vary physically according to circumstance and function. This is so much more powerful than simply doing letter layout, partly because the context here is enjoyable, not dry, and partly because the variety of texts means that pupils are necessarily making comparisons, and comparisons lead to understanding at a fundamental level. They will see that texts vary because they have to in order to function as they need to. I've seen many solemn lessons on business-letter layout, but I don't think I've ever seen any discussion of why it is as it is, or why that matters.

When the file is finished, the documents are assembled in a folder, in the correct order, so that a reader can follow the story without needing a word of narrative. The murderer's name is in a sealed envelope. Pupils swap folders and solve each other's crimes, and this involves a relevant and organic peer evaluation (see Chapter 6). This scheme of work is guaranteed to absorb and extend pupils in Year 8 or Year 9.

Slightly controversial views on homework

My progress in chemistry was partly impeded by the fact that I spent a proportion of the lessons in the boys' toilets because I hadn't done my homework and was scared of Mr Webster. I still have profoundly mixed feelings about the value of homework, partly because it can

create a barrier between pupil and teacher, and partly because the work itself is often not well planned, explained or understood. Homework is necessary (although I don't know how you would explain to a Martian that children in our civilised society are forced to work all day and all night as well); it's popular with parents, politicians and many teachers; but it needs to be used wisely and appropriately.

Homework should occur within the context and momentum of classwork, but, ideally, it should also exploit its own particular opportunities, not simply attempt to be a continuation of school. It provides new contacts, contexts and audiences to extend the learning. For example, a pupil could:

- measure and describe her house (for a sales brochure);
- re-decorate her bedroom (writing instructions);

- set a story in her garden (understanding how fiction makes use of reality);
- interview her dad about fox-hunting (to help prepare a debate speech);
- survey her family;
- analyse a TV programme;
- carry out a radio survey in connection with media study;
- analyse a soap opera for dramatic irony;
- describe her street using personification;
- look at family language.

Setting large chunks of pseudo-classwork (reading or writing) may be necessary at times, but it isn't the best use of the potential of homework, and needs careful setting up and monitoring. It should be explained as carefully as any other tasks, not set in a hurry at the end of the lesson, and evaluated in ways that avoid massive policing sessions at the beginnings of lessons and unrealistic marking loads for yourself. Homework doesn't always require written outcomes; it can be monitored through discussion, for example. If pupils are doing large writing homeworks (for example, in preparing examination coursework) then they need highly structured tasks and supports. A homework essay on *whether war is ever justified* will only be worth doing if discursive planning (not just war discussion) has formed a significant part of your classroom work, so that pupils carry home a scaffold, not just a task. Even then, you should be aware of the law of diminishing returns when relying on homework to cover significant amounts of the curriculum. An important choice about homework is whether it looks back to the previous lesson (finishing off, consolidating, extending) or forward to the next one (research, preparation). You will set both, but you need to remember the value and liveliness of the second kind.

Look at the planning first

When you are trying to solve problems in your teaching, start by looking at your planning. If pupils aren't listening, aren't under-standing, aren't behaving, aren't settling or aren't turning up, the problem is probably solved in the planning. For example, if a class is unruly, it's tempting to become involved in critical analysis of your classroom performance, voice, body language and relationships and to embark on complex sanctions procedures. Any of this may be productive, but in my experience the problem often lies in the work itself. Inappropriate levels, access routes, explanations, instructions and material will ensure that pupil attitude degenerates. Often the required adjustments are quite straightforward and the improvements are likely to be sustained.

Organise

I recently asked my teacher-training students to write down one single important development in terms of their progress; one wrote, *I bought a filing cabinet*. Half of the stress of teaching can be removed by good organisation. You can't rely on charisma and innate genius. If you claim that natural flair means you can get away with organisational sloppiness, perhaps believing, as I did for years, that this makes you more intriguing and attractive, you're only fooling yourself. The less organised you are, the more organised you have to be. Colour code different classes. Mark up your own weekly timetable with fixed spaces for setting and marking homework, allowing you to stagger marking for different classes. The managerial aspects of teaching are formidable and if you don't pay attention to them, a timebomb is surely ticking. And planning is the most important thing a teacher does.

Chapter 3

Learning to love objectives

The teacher was doing the book-cover lesson. You know it well; you did it at school; I have taught it twenty times. He had prepared it carefully: he had shown them the particular bit of origami that transforms a piece of A4 into something unconvincingly resembling a book jacket; he had made an elaborate diagram on the board labelling the components such as *plot blurb, author's biography, picture.* Year 8 were making book covers for the class reader, *The Ghost of Thomas Kempe.*

It should have been a lively, successful lesson; felt-tip pens were involved. I was sitting at the back, watching the naughty boys swinging backwards on their chairs, the two cross frustrated girls in front of me who wanted to work in a more productive atmosphere, watching the behaviour and commitment deteriorate from minute to minute, wondering exactly why it was all so pointless.

It was a key moment for me. For twenty years I had been a successful English teacher who, like all the colleagues I knew at that time, didn't ever think in terms of learning objectives. They have never been popular with English teachers. We like to explore, we value the unexpected; the objective sits on the lesson like the cold hand of bureaucracy, inorganic, inhibiting creativity. Even now, with the *Framework* lying at the heart of English teaching, learning objectives give rise to deep suspicion.

The book-cover teacher had some management skills; he wasn't without presence; he had prepared the lesson. But as I watched him, I realised that he had no idea of what he was teaching. The lesson had no purpose or focus, though it looked busy enough. In the *Learning Objectives* box on his lesson plan, he had written, *The pupils will make book covers.*

Children don't go to school to do things; they go to school to learn things. If you are still defining a lesson by what will happen in it, rather than what pupils will learn from it, you are still planning from activities. The day you move to planning from objectives your teaching will undergo a step-change in focus and coherence. Lessons will grow around activities which are linked and progressive; they will become easier to plan; they will make more sense to pupils, who will remember what they've learned.

There are, after all, many valuable learning opportunities in the book-cover lesson or the poster lesson or the web-site lesson. At the base of them is purpose and audience. What is the purpose of the book cover? The teacher had made only the most cursory references to purpose; he said that the cover illustrates, decorates and "provides information about" the book, with no sense at all of why anybody should want to do any of that, or for whom. Failing to see the potential of the work in terms of purpose and audience was a fatal error resulting from activity-based planning, from *thinking about what they would do rather than why they were doing it or what they would learn.* None of the subsequent activities had any direction because of this fundamental flaw, this objectives vacuum at the heart of the work.

The audience of the book cover is in fact a potential buyer, and its purpose is to attract him and persuade him to buy. The book cover is an advertisement; its function lives and dies on the bookshop shelf.

Every decision about it rests on this, but the lesson reflected none of it. For example, the children were encouraged to write a plot blurb for the book. They were told that this is a paragraph which sums up the story, for the reader's information. Thus they set off on the almost entirely worthless and wholly tedious task of summarising a novel in one paragraph with no sense of what to include and what to leave out and why.

This failure to begin from the objective of understanding the purpose and audience removes value and richness from every part of the lesson. It means that the blurb is wrongly cast as a plot summary, when in fact it should be a *partial, selective, distorted summary* cunningly constructed to persuade the reader to buy the novel. A full plot summary is in fact the last thing the publisher wants on the book cover. How many copies of Agatha Christie novels would be sold on this basis? The blurb only tells you enough to make you want more. Its function is to persuade, not to inform.

Consider the real value of a lesson in which children think about how to write a truly persuasive blurb. The teacher shows them examples of blurbs on other novels, perhaps in the library. They discuss them in groups, deciding from their blurbs which books they would choose, and thus arriving at some criteria for evaluating an effective blurb in terms of persuasive content, tone and language. Then, in pairs, they discuss which bits of *The Ghost of Thomas Kempe* should be included in a blurb, which bits should be exaggerated, and which bits should be tantalisingly left out.

This is now a high-level discussion covering various literacy objectives, creative and analytical, and resulting in collaborative writing with clear direction. It is interesting to pupils because it allows them to form and enact their opinions about the book. It happens because the teacher has planned not from an activity, but from a learning objective, such as *Pupils will understand the persuasive purpose of a blurb and how this affects its tone and content*, and this probably links the lesson to others using entirely different kinds of material to further examine persuasive language in other contexts. A good blurb, properly discussed and understood, is worth a whole wall-display of book covers.

A teacher who sees *Make a book cover* as an objective is not seeing the many challenging and differing language opportunities the pupil will be encountering and is unlikely to be giving proper value to any one of them. Such a lesson is likely to fall apart. Consider the many skills and concepts involved. They might include:

- writing an advertising blurb (*language to persuade, emotive language, language for a particular audience*);
- writing a selective plot synopsis (*literary response and comprehension, tone, selection of appropriate material, summary*);
- designing artwork (*literary response, selection of appropriate characters and scenes, awareness of visual qualities in the writing*);
- writing author's biography (*research, factual language*);
- writing "review extracts" (*hyperbole, succinctness, subjectivity*).

While a literate adult may see no problem in integrating these varied language activities, a child needs each one to be decontextualised, discussed, exemplified, demonstrated, and re-contextualised. The list above has too many potential learning objectives, and this is another highly significant step forward for many teachers – the need to cover much less much better.

Line-by-line, verse-by-verse

I recently watched two consecutive lessons (taught by two consecutive teachers) which provided a telling illustration of the need to plan to objectives which are few and small. The more local and specific the objective, the better. In the first lesson, the teacher did a poem. "Doing" a text consists of working through it giving notes, having discussions, trying to make it interesting as you go along. I taught like this for many years. The poem on this occasion was by Wilfred Owen and the teacher and pupils worked manfully through it. After about half an hour, they had notes on the First World War, Owen, the sonnet form, alliteration, onomatopoeia, rhyme and rhythm, the meanings of various new words in the poem, symbolism, metaphor, assonance, bathos and irony. These things had cropped up as they went along and the teacher had made a reasonable job of explaining them.

The chances of the children remembering all or most of this learning and being able to reapply it in the future are slim. Almost any one of these concepts is worthy of being properly taught, from the context of the poem, using other examples, using creativity and analysis. *At the planning stage, you have to decide whether you're going to teach eight things of which the pupils will forget four and confuse the rest, or whether you're going to teach one or two things well.* A lesson which began from the notion that Owen's poetry makes telling use of onomatopoeia (for example) would build towards an understanding of the term through consideration of onomatopoeia in jokes, newspaper headlines, other poems and the pupils' own creative writing. It would compare onomatopoeic writing with non-onomatopoeic equivalencies to appreciate its effects. It would take time to present multiple approaches to the understanding. And it would not limit the pupils' responses to the poem as a whole, because onomatopoeia would be discussed in terms of its effects on the reader, its contribution to the emotional vividness of Owen's language.

This emphatically doesn't mean that the understanding of poetry lies in the forensic examination of the text against a series of techniques. I have sat and shuddered when hearing a teacher, having just read aloud a poem, say, "The first thing I want you to do is to underline all the similes." There is a belief that poetry differs from other text types because it's susceptible to systematic technical analysis – there are even acronym-based systems for this. Technical issues should never be *the first thing*: personal response should always in some way be the first thing; and when it's time to analyse personal response in terms of the writer's methods, techniques need to be selectively and deeply explored.

It's quite brave, in fact, to plan to few and small objectives. *Doing a poem* is comforting to the teacher: it feels rigorous; the pupils have lots of notes and, apparently, learn lots of new things. To decide that real understanding of one or two key concepts is more worthwhile than pebbledash coverage means a commitment to the pupils' long-term learning rather than the teacher's short-term sense of well-being. On the same day I watched a lesson on Act 3, Scene 5 of *Romeo and Juliet*. The scene features ambiguity. Juliet is talking to her mother about her forbidden love for Romeo, but her mother thinks she's talking about her grief over the death of her cousin Tybalt. Juliet deliberately hides behind this misunderstanding. She isn't lying to her mother, but she isn't telling the truth, either.

The teacher had decided not to "do" the scene but to *build the whole lesson around the single objective that pupils would understand its ambiguity*. In fact, there are two objectives – to understand the concept of ambiguity, and then to see it in the conversation between the Capulet women. What looks at first sight like a single objective is often in fact several – the concept must be understood, and then its use in the given context must be appreciated. These activities are not identical. Of course the text provides the context for the generic understanding, but your planning has to take account of this complexity and take pupils stage-by-stage to real understanding. In this case, the teacher had decided that, if the pupils could leave the room understanding ambiguity and its power in this scene, were able to explain it to their mums at home and to remember it in three days' time, then that would be an hour well spent.

Once you have this central objective, the lesson is easy to plan. Objectives are your planning friends. From one single idea, the teacher constructed a lesson which began with a discussion of a scene from *Home and Away* in which deliberate ambiguity featured, followed by a paired role play in which pupil A (teenager) had to convince pupil B (parent) that she wasn't going to a party at her friend's house, even though she was. She had to do this without lying, under some quite fierce questioning (*Will there be lots of people there? Well, a few of my friends . . .*) So, at the key transition points between such activities, the notion of ambiguity becomes explicit and roundly understood, and the pupils recognise it when they read the (appropriately edited) scene from Shakespeare.

The pebbledash teacher who wants to explain everything in the scene will say that this approach doesn't provide enough learning, there's too much to get through to spend an hour on one or two ideas; and his pupils will go on making notes on a dozen things a day and when later asked what onomatopoeia is they will hesitate and then tentatively assert that it might be the one where all the words begin with the same letter.

Of course, focusing on one, two or three key objectives isn't limiting. The pupils are still learning about the plot of the play and the relationships within it; but the objectives provide a coherent narrative to the stages of the lesson, which gives them confidence. Because they understand ambiguity, they understand the scene; the objective is like a torch in the darkness, allowing the pupils to move forward and see more and more. A lesson is a journey: it should leave pupils in a new place. The lesson plan is a sketch map for the journey, and *the objective is the destination, the first planning consideration, not an afterthought*. Naturally, this doesn't mean that, in the event, you can't take a more attractive route, at a different speed, and stop to admire an unexpected view.

Small is beautiful

Objectives should help you to plan. They enable focus and coherence within and across lessons. They come from different places; many of them probably originate in the *Framework* or in GCSE or post-16 specifications. They tend to be wordy, generic statements. If they are to be helpful to you, they have to be brought down to size and rendered highly specific, friendly, and local to your teaching. They have to become yours.

Typically, you will have a medium- or short-term plan in front of you when you come to plan your lesson. This will provide content and objectives to go with it; but the lesson plan itself remains your own. This is where you have freedom not only to devise activities but to *tame and recast the generalised objective in useful and specific terms*.

You may be looking at Martin Luther King's *I have a dream . . .* speech as part of a medium-term plan on persuasive language. This is an extraordinary text and, in its time, a dangerously powerful one. The planned *Framework* objective for this Year 8 work could be *analyse the overall structure of a text to identify how key ideas are developed, e.g. through the organisation of the content and the patterns of language used*.

This is a typical *Framework* objective and, in terms of Martin Luther King, it isn't irrelevant. However, even despite its examples, it isn't especially helpful to your planning. It explains why you're reading King, but it offers few thoughts on what you might actually do with him on a Thursday afternoon. You need to supplement the generalised objective with a specific one of your own. You need to decide which *content* and *patterns* of the speech can be appreciated by your Year 8 pupils, and which might best be left. For example, while looking at

> Five score years ago, a great American, in whose symbolic shadow we stand, signed the Emancipation Proclamation. This momentous decree came as a great beacon light of hope to millions of Negro slaves who had been seared in the flames of withering injustice. It came as a joyous daybreak to end the long night of captivity. But one hundred years later, we must face the tragic fact that the Negro is still not free.
>
> One hundred years later, the life of the Negro is still sadly crippled by the manacles of segregation and the chains of discrimination. One hundred years later, the Negro lives on a lonely island of poverty in the midst of a vast ocean of material prosperity. One hundred years later, the Negro is still languishing in the corners of American society and finds himself an exile in his own land.
>
> So we have come here today to dramatize an appalling condition. In a sense we have come to our nation's capital to cash a check. When the architects of our republic wrote the magnificent words of the Constitution and the Declaration of Independence, they were signing a promissory note to which every American was to fall heir . . .

you might decide that they will respond to key features such as the repetition (of various phrases, not just the keynote line), the sustained metaphors (for example, the metaphor of the cheque) and the strong, figurative language. You might on the other hand decide that the powerful use of antithesis will be too challenging for them at this stage. You are making decisions about how to focus the objectives.

So your lesson will begin with two main objectives: the given *Framework* objective and the specific, local rendering of that, which might be *Pupils will understand and appreciate King's use of repe-*

tition and metaphor. This second objective sounds less grand than the first, but it grows from it, and it provides a basis for planning activities.

For example, this is a speech, so a strong thing to do with it is to read it aloud to a class who cannot see it (or allow them to see the text but then require them immediately to turn it over so they can't take a second look), and then ask them to write down what they remember. After all, King's audience only heard it once. Pupils will immediately respond to key rhetorical features through this simple memory device and this can begin your discussion of the power of repetition which will go into and beyond the speech itself.

The paradox of the general and the specific

Good objectives are specific and local. Traditionally, they denote what children will learn, understand or be able to do by the end of the lesson. Think while planning not only of 0 to 60 (they leave after an hour with something they didn't come in with) but also of 0 to 24 (what will they remember tomorrow?) An objective which says *Pupils will appreciate the characteristics of persuasive language* is far from meaningless but it's nowhere near as helpful as *Pupils will understand euphemism and how estate agents use it in their brochures.*

But there is a paradox here because one of the main values of objectives is that they allow for generic paths and links among the learning, both within individual lessons and across whole schemes of work. In practice, the more specific the objective the more successful the learning, and so the more effectively it can transfer to and be developed in subsequent teaching. *If you make the objective highly specific it can then be generalised into other contexts.* So, ono-matopoeia, ambiguity, mystery, the rhetorical effects of repetition, the misleading use of euphemism, once explored, can be transferred to new contexts.

Triangulate to accumulate

In fact, the use of more contexts than the immediate one is highly beneficial to the learning, and objective-based planning encourages this. Brilliant teachers triangulate from an objective, which is just a fancy way of saying they go to three places. There's (1) the euphemism in the estate agents' brochures which you're studying; then there's (2) euphemism in other places introduced by you and perhaps the pupils in discussion; and (3) the euphemisms that the pupils write for themselves to show they've got the point (and to enjoy its sneakiness). Many teachers just stop at (1), but the range of contexts in (2) and (3) is very powerful indeed. It allows multiple approaches to the concept; it shows that the concept exists in the world, not just the lesson; it encourages pupils to re-apply the concept and so really get to use it.

Some myths about objectives

It's very difficult to think them up

The objective is what the children learn. If this isn't the basis of your teaching, what is? But objectives don't have to sound grand, general and academic, and the most useful ones don't.

They spoil spontaneity

They provide focus and continuity, but any lesson can undergo radical changes in the delivery. The ones that do are sometimes the best ones.

You can teach perfectly well without them

This can never be true – how can you teach without planning for pupil learning? But it's interesting to consider why it gets said. Experienced teachers say it; I thought it myself for many years. The fact is that good teaching often gets done by teachers who are using objectives implicitly. They devise activities which produce good learning and already have a sense of what pupils are getting out of them. Their good teaching will become even better when they recognise that they are already using objectives and begin to plan explicitly around them.

You have to write them on the board at the start of every lesson

You should always know and plan from your objectives, but your lesson plan might not require the pupils to know them from the start. Lessons should often have an air of exploration; pupils are working towards the objectives, not recovering from an initial definition of them. In fact the mechanistic reputation of objectives may stem from the rigid lesson shape which demands their initial publication on the board and final evaluation where pupils dutifully report at the end of the lesson that they have, indeed, learned what they should have. Sometimes, if the lesson is a story, the objectives are the hidden treasure.

They are utilitarian

Many objectives are technical, but they don't have to be. In teaching Browning's *My Last Duchess* one of my objectives is that pupils recognise the mystery at the heart of the poem. This allows me to plan an active lesson in which the Duke is put on trial for his wife's murder, using evidence and inference from the poem, analysing its central mystery. It also gives me a direct path to an apparently very different poem, Auden's *O What is That Sound?*, which also depends for its energy on a central ambiguity. By looking at such an objective across these two apparently quite different contexts, we can begin to form judgments about some of the things that poetry does.

You don't need them with sixth-formers

Of course, post-16 teaching is different. The pupils are volunteers: they love the subject; they love learning; you don't need to plan systematically; all you need is a gas fire, some marshmallows to toast, and a schooner of medium-dry sherry to sip as they read their essays aloud in the darkening afternoon.

You may have noticed that this is a fantasy, but it's not an uncommon one. Post-16 teaching requires all of the planning, structure and focus of the rest of your work. It certainly requires local and specific learning objectives, and here as elsewhere they are a support to collaborative and focused teaching. The line-by-line approach is especially tempting and especially unproductive at this level. Clear objectives provide structures for lessons which generate discussion and understanding. There are many possibilities in Chapter 1 of *Wuthering Heights*, but having a simple, clear objective like drawing initial conclusions about the similarities and differences between Heathcliff and Lockwood will provide a focus for reading and a structure (two columns) for note-making and discussion. A brilliant teacher always finds a learning objective. The answer to *Why are you reading Chapter 17* today? has to be an answer that relates to this – *Because we can focus on the writer's introduction of a new character in this chapter*, for example. *Because we read Chapter 16 yesterday* isn't really going to help your planning.

Chapter 4

Poetry, small texts and pupil responses

Poetry seems to polarise teachers. Some love to teach it; others think that pupils have a particular dislike of it. Perhaps the problem is the odd, other-worldly status we seem to afford it. The *poetry voice*, for example, has turned whole generations of children against poetry. You remember it: you take a deep breath and read the poem as though it were in a slightly foreign language, half a note above your usual pitch, in a kind of strangulated monotone, and this confers a kind of dignity on the whole thing. Unfortunately, it also removes most of its meaning and alienates your audience, confirming that poetry is something that exists on a non-human plane and is far too good for the likes of them.

Texts, literary or non-literary, are collections of words that seek to affect the reader through their meanings and other dynamic qualities, and the starting point for pupils in understanding how they work lies in their effects. Good teachers work with authors' intentions, but brilliant teachers understand that, while they don't have the author in the classroom, they do have the readers, and *readers are central to the process.*

Building the confidence of your readers in their own responses is the most significant part of building textual analysis, and brilliant teachers make this an explicit process, a learning objective in itself. When we ask pupils for their initial responses to a poem, for example, they will try all kinds of things, including finding didactic messages where there aren't any, panicking because there are lines they don't understand, spotting all the similes, counting the rhyme scheme, and so on. They will also immediately self-censor, ignoring a range of other reactions that they think are incorrect or impertinent. They might think the poem stupid, or boring, or frankly incomprehensible, or funny when it's clearly not meant to be; they probably won't own

up to any of this. This distortion of their reaction is damaging, and it proceeds from a lack of confidence. Building confidence means that *all* responses must be acknowledged and validated, because all responses are useful.

Here is a process that illustrates this. The lesson centres on William Blake's *The Sick Rose*, and it is for an able Year 10, 11 or 12 group, though it is a process that could be applied very widely. While the lesson will certainly proceed to an understanding of the poem, its prime objective is to build reader confidence.

> O Rose, thou art sick!
> The invisible worm
> That flies in the night
> In the howling storm
>
> Has found out thy bed
> Of crimson joy,
> And his dark, secret love
> Doth thy life destroy.

When you read a poem like this and ask for reactions, children will immediately self-censor. They won't indicate if they find the poem stupid, or boring. Such reactions get ignored; but they may well be the first and most genuine impressions of the poem, its initial and powerful effect on its readers, and the brilliant teacher stays with these reactions and, in fact, uses them to unlock the text.

Difficulty and the *stupid syndrome*

What these subversive reactions are saying, in their different ways, is that the pupil finds the poem difficult. The "stupid syndrome" often kicks in here – the pupil emphatic that either the poet is stupid ("Why doesn't he say what he means?"), the teacher is stupid ("Why do we have to read this stuff?") or the pupil himself is too stupid to grasp it. It's a common way of fending off difficulty.

But difficulty is very often the first reaction – after all, we expect to be challenging our pupils; and we should embrace it, rather than evading it. The point of this lesson is that the difficulty, far from preventing us from understanding, will actually help us towards it.

So we agree with our pupils that the poem is difficult. We don't pretend otherwise. This agreement is in itself powerful in building confidence – difficulty becomes a shared part of the study rather then a personal failure. One way forward is to make the poem less difficult by explaining it. Another might be "background", with lots of Blake engravings and Romantic theory. *The best way, though, is to accept this as a valid literary response, in itself a genuine insight, and to begin to analyse it.*

The key exploration is to answer the key question – *why* is the poem difficult? Pupils can be guided to an answer by considering various possibilities. For example, is the vocabulary difficult? The hardest word in the poem is *invisible*. So pupils can now be helped to write, *The poem is difficult despite its simple vocabulary*. Because, not despite of, their initial negative reaction, they have now made a valid critical statement.

The process can be repeated, for example with structure and grammar. It is a very simple poem. So pupils can write, *The poem is complicated despite its simple vocabulary, conventional structure and straightforward grammar*. Their initial response, far from being censored or ignored, is still there, driving their work. This is one stage in building confidence.

In this discussion of what is and is not difficult, the pupils will work towards the central problem of who or what Rose is. Arguments will break out. Some will insist that she's a girl, with a capital letter and a girl's name. In this case the *worm* might be a disease, or sexual corruption. Others will admit with embarrassment that they took Rose literally to be a flower with some sort of canker. So the poem's central difficulty is finally laid bare. Is Rose a girl or a flower? (*Bed* is a fascinating word in this context – a flowerbed or a sickbed or something more sexual?)

By examining their first reactions to the poem's difficulty, the pupils have come to an understanding of its central dynamic, which is its ambiguity. It's difficult because it's ambiguous. Rather than trying to resolve this ambiguity, the teacher steers the conversation towards accepting it. The stupid syndrome may rear its head here – *why* is the poem ambiguous? Why isn't it clear what Rose is? Which is she, anyway? Who's right?

These typical questions arise from an ethos dealing with author's intention. Some texts, such as the RSPCA leaflet that sets out to raise awareness through shocking images of animal cruelty, will have clear intentions and are susceptible to a *purpose-and-audience* approach. In many such cases, authors' intentions and effects on reader are almost synonymous for our purposes. But we can't be entirely sure of Blake's intentions in writing this confusing poem. What we can be sure of is how it affects us.

When pupils stop worrying about their confusion and allow it into their imaginations they can begin to look directly at their responses. They should be encouraged to view their own reactions, as a cinema screen in their heads. Often they will see the girl Rose and the flower together; in their confusion, they will imagine the one and then the other; the two images will be almost superimposed. When they see that this, *far from being a failure to understand or solve the problem, is in fact the poem's central energy*, their impressions all through the process are vindicated. It is difficult because it is confusing, and this fuses the poem's imagery into a picture of decay and natural transience, where a girl's beauty and purity are no more permanent or secure than the blossoming of a flower. Their difficulty took them to the poem's essential metaphor.

It takes confidence for a pupil to accept that something is difficult without consequently rejecting it (the stupid syndrome), and this confidence grows in the ethos that values reader reaction at least as highly as writer intention. In fact there is a sense in which textual appreciation for any secondary age group consists in answering two questions:

* What effect does this text have on me?
* How is the effect created?

The leaflet might revolt you, the poem confuse you, the report clarify things for you, the newspaper article annoy you, the short story amuse you: whatever the effect, pupils should begin their studies there, rather than with second-guessing the motives of an unknown and unseen author.

The absolute fundamental crucial centrality of comparison in understanding text effects – please do not skip this section

You might remember comparison as an awful sort of literary chore – Blake vs. Wordsworth, the broadsheet and the tabloid, compare and contrast two poems about a fish. I want to argue here however that comparison is *absolutely fundamental* to building text response, that it should be used constantly, lesson on lesson, probably several times in each lesson, and that the opportunities for it are many and easy, though it is frequently ignored.

I'm not talking here though about formal compare-and-contrast procedures but about the fact that children can't be expected to appreciate a textual effect without a point of comparison, and that point of comparison is, at its simplest, *the text as it might have been without the effect in question.* This moment of comparison, which can be quite brief, is the moment when real appreciation happens. It is the essential closing of a teaching-and-learning loop but, time after time, it's a loop that's left open. Brilliant teachers complete this cycle explicitly.

For example, you might be looking at a passage of fiction like this one:

> At first, he could see and hear nothing; he began to wonder why he'd climbed in through that broken window in the first place, with its jagged edges and (even more worryingly) its massive spider webs. He crouched by the wall in the dark, thinking about getting out again.
>
> And then he heard it. A movement. A scuffling. Something was breathing. He held his own breath. He peered into the darkness. He could see nothing. But the breathing was getting closer.

You might be making the fair point that suspense is caused in part by the short sentences in the second paragraph. A good teacher may spend some time on creative writing here, with children perhaps trying their own sentence-length variations in their own stories; you could build this into a *What happens next?* game as pupils read out their own suspense passages and the class guesses the outcomes. They will in these ways begin to understand that short sentences can add to the tension.

However, the most convincing argument is the comparison of the text as it is with the text as it might have been. Once you have the alternative

> And then he heard a movement and a scuffling. Something was breathing, and so he held his own breath but, peering into the darkness, he could see nothing, although the breathing was getting closer.

you can *see*, *feel* and *believe* the difference. In fact you can carry the learning further by beginning to understand in more detail why the short sentences are so effective. You can discuss for example the padding, plodding effect of the conjunctions in the second version. *This comparison is essential to complete the understanding.* As graduates, we are expert readers with a huge automatic comparison database; we are comparing subliminally all the time to make sense of and judgments about what we read. *Children need this essential habit to be made explicit.*

But often this final stage is left out completely, even though it's so easy to do. The children can write the second version themselves, exploring different ways of linking the short sentences; and then, in pairs, they can compare the original with their transformations. This short-sentences work is now building nicely into a brief sequence of comparative exercises, including text transformation and creative writing, which will generate genuine understanding of writers' choices and their effects on readers. The work centres on a clear and local objective. It's more elaborate than the teacher simply making the point and moving on; in terms of 0–24, it is likely to be retained for use in the future.

These moments of comparison, however, don't need to be even as elaborate as that. Indeed, they need to be habitual, which means they need to be immediately, spontaneously available to the teacher. So, when a teacher makes the point that, when a poet says

> He made me feel he was all ready to
> Eat me. And any girl enjoys that

the word *Eat* receives a telling, rather sexy emphasis because it's been placed at the beginning of a line, it should be habit to have the pupils jot the line without the line break

> He made me feel he was all ready to eat me . . .

and to talk about the difference. It's a visual difference; they need to see it. Without this moment (less than a minute of your lesson) pupils will accept that *Eat* is emphasised as you say (as they will accept that Lima is the capital of Peru) but they may not feel it.

These should become teaching and learning habits. Pupils should be so used to being urged to make these comparisons that they make them without being asked, as part of their usual note-making. I was recently making some points to a Year 12 group about half-rhymes. They couldn't see why a poet would choose to not quite hit the rhymes properly and I was saying that the half-rhymes created a sense of incompleteness which added to a kind of sadness in the poem. They looked at me indulgently, prepared to forgive (and also to forget) my whimsy until I had them rewrite a few lines with full-on, simplistic rhymes and compare the effects of the two. Immediately the penny began to drop.

This kind of straightforward comparison strengthens the teaching of virtually any effect, at word, sentence or text level. It is always available and always necessary. You can tell pupils that alliteration adds energy to a tabloid headline but they'll only fully believe it when they rewrite the headline without it and talk about the difference between BEN'S LARGE PARTY and BEN'S BIGGEST BONANZA. Rewriting an estate agent's brochure with honest translations of its euphemisms and then doing the comparison will make explicit points which guarantee understanding.

At text level, this comparative process can make themes and attitudes come alive. It's fine to compare the *Londons* of Blake and Wordsworth, much more than twice as effective as reading only one of them; but even when there isn't an obvious comparative, the lesson can generate one. I spent years telling pupils that Keats' *Ode to Autumn* is an exciting poem that is actually quite radical. Twenty-first-century kids really can't see this; what they see is a biscuit-tin-lid painting, corny in more ways than one. "It's really quite a surprising view of Autumn," I would say, and they would say, "Yeah, astonishing."

It was a simple matter to provide the essential comparison. We collaborated on key autumn words *before reading the poem* – we filled the board with *mud, slush, rain, wind, death, dead leaves, drizzle, decay, darkness, rot, toadstools* . . . Against this we read the poem and saw how systematically Keats converts these negatives to positives – *season of mists*, not *season of fogs*. You create an expectation and then the point you're trying to make takes on some sort of life in contrast with it. I don't suppose they talked about it on the bus that night ("You'll never guess what Keats says, it's really quite astonishing . . ."), but they certainly understood the difference.

Don't ditch DARTs

(or, without the alliteration, Remember DARTs . . .)

So it's helpful to consider that *every response is a sort of comparison*, and the brilliant teacher is aware of this at all times and writes it explicitly into the planning, giving it space and structure to be complete. I have watched lesson after lesson where central activities give rise to comparative opportunities that are not exploited. Three-quarters of the learning isn't much better than no learning at all.

Take deletions, for example. Filling in the blanks is an excellent thing to be doing; DARTs of this kind are marvellous focusing devices and if you're inclined to dismiss them you should try doing some yourself. You will find that you engage with the text at a new level. For example, I often teach the John Donne sonnet *Death be Not Proud* by simply deleting the word *Death* throughout. When using deletions, you must (as always) be absolutely clear what your objective is, and in this case I want to show how odd Donne's treatment is. He uses personification, and by doing this he reduces Death to the extent that, finally, he can become more powerful than it. Of course, I can tell them this; I can "do" the poem and they can make notes on that process; in some sense, they will understand it, but they are a long way from seeing how odd or radical or successful this is. Perhaps every new piece of reading should be a small shock.

> — be not proud, though some have called thee
> Mighty and dreadfull, for, thou art not so,
> For, those, whom thou think'st, thou dost overthrow,
> Die not, poore —, nor yet canst thou kill me.
> From rest and sleepe, which but thy pictures bee,
> Much pleasure, then from thee, much more must flow,
> And soonest our best men with thee doe goe,
> Rest of their bones, and soules deliverie.
> Thou art slave to Fate, Chance, kings, and desperate men,
> And dost with poyson, warre, and sicknesse dwell,
> And poppie, or charmes can make us sleepe as well,
> And better then thy stroake; why swell'st thou then;
> One short sleepe past, wee wake eternally,
> And — shall be no more; —, thou shalt die.

When children do the deletions, a few will come up with *death*, but most will find other words. *King*, *Lord* and *God* are not uncommon. What happens next is crucial, and this is where it so often goes wrong.

Do you remember lessons like this? The teacher distributes the poem with the blanks. The children fill them in. There follows the "auction" period of the lesson where the teacher works through the poem and children put their hands up, vying to be right, cheering when they are. Their suggestions are discussed until the correct answers are finally listed on the board; the children can then fill them in and probably everybody feels that something has been achieved. But the central purpose of the activity hasn't even been approached.

A DART like this is only effective when properly understood, used and exploited. For example, in discussing the Donne, the children will offer words which describe people – king, etc. – in place of Death, so that personification becomes a reality for them. They will see that the syntax and tone of the poem turn Death into a person, *because that's what they did*. They will also begin to understand the force of the final paradox – that Death will die. Of course you can just read it and tell them that it's a paradox; but when children look at their own versions – *King, thou shalt die, Lord, thou shalt die* – and compare them with Donne they will appreciate how unlikely the paradox is. They didn't anticipate it; there's a kind of impossibility about it; they know this, *because they ruled it out for themselves*. There is a deeper understanding here, but only when these comparative discussions reach their explicit conclusions and the circles are carefully closed.

What to do and what not to do with DARTs

They're DARTs, not ARTs, and the *Direction* is crucial. It's usually better to do a DART than to "do" a poem – but there's no point in "doing" a DART either without really knowing why. I've seen this countless times. the teacher has to analyse a report or an article or a poem, so he "does" deletions, or sequencing. In planning, he begins with the text, then moves on to an activity, when he should have begun with an objective. He runs the "auction" lesson mentioned above and the activity certainly does provoke close textual discussion; but it has no real focus and veers towards a conclusion which supplies the right answers and proves once again that the author knows best, and guessing his intentions is the real and only response to his work.

A competent teacher does a poem, a good teacher does a DART, and a brilliant teacher uses a DART to enhance pupil response in connection with an appropriate objective. In U. A. Fanthorpe's *Horticultural Show* I want the pupils to appreciate how eery and yet accurate are the descriptions of the vegetables. I delete all the vegetables, and the pupils work in pairs and decide on vegetables of their own. Usually they get about half of them right. Here's the poem. Every gap is a removed vegetable, except for the last one.

These are Persephone's fruits
Of the underyear. These will guide us
Through the slow dream of winter.

— her paleskinned lamps.
Rub them for strange knowledge. They shine
With the light of the tomb.

Drawn in fine runes along
Hard green rinds, the incomprehensible
Initiation of the —.

All orange energy driven
Down to a final hair, these —
Have been at the heart of darkness.

And parti-coloured —,
Their green hair plaited, like Iroquois braves,
Leaning exhausted in corners.

Holystoned the presence
Of —, pure white and stained pink.
Persephone's bread.

Sacrificed —
Display their bleeding hearts. We read
The future in these entrails.

Out in the world excitable
Ponies caper, Punch batters Judy, a man
Creates a drystone wall in thirty minutes,

Arrows fly, coconuts fall, crocodiles
And jubilee mugs, disguised as children,
Cope with candyfloss, the band
Adds its slow waltz heart beat.

Here in the tent, in the sepia hush,
Persephone's fruits utter where they have been,
Where — are going.

Crucial things happen to give this lesson purpose and structure and to provide the essential opportunities for comparison which will build pupils' responses.

Firstly, I have a clear objective; I'm not just doing the deletions for the sake of it, or for fun, but because I want the pupils to recognise certain aspects of the writing. They will do this through a process of surprise and discovery. I have imagined at the planning stage the kinds of discussions the activity is likely to provoke. I want them to see how weird and unexpected the descriptions are.

Secondly, they will work in pairs. DARTs are almost always best in pairs. There needs to be close textual discussion (not so easy in large groups) but there also needs to be comparison, trial, improvement, creative testing (not so easy on your own). So they will discuss and argue about the text as they make creative decisions. Of course, this process is far more important than the "answers" they come up with later.

Thirdly, there is no sense at all of "right answers". Of course pupils will want to know what the writer said, but this must always be part

of a process of comparison. Pupil contributions are equally significant. So often I've seen the lesson move quickly to the auction which,
like all auctions, is highly competitive, with clear rewards going to
those who match the author.

In fact, you usually don't want them to match the author. If they
do, the activity probably hasn't challenged them. You want them to
find alternatives, because their alternatives provide the basis for the
essential comparisons. *This is the most important feature of the lesson
but very often it is completely left out.*

The key resolution of the DART lesson is the comparison, and
you must structure this activity with just as much care as the DART
itself. The learning lies not in their getting it right, nor even in the
nature of their suggestions; it lies in the comparison of those suggestions with the original text. So, for example, in the *Horticultural
Show* lesson, the pupils proceed from the deletions to a structured
comparison, basing their discussion on a simple prompt sheet such
as this such as Table 4.1 below:

The DART-led comparison is taking this Year 9 pupil towards a
sense of the unreal and bizarrely mystical quality of Fanthorpe's
writing. She is beginning to understand how the particular quality
of the poem has something to do with the journey from pumpkins
to onions. *Without the banality of the pumpkins, she can't appreciate
the oddness of the onions.*

Table 4.1 Using deletions

Deletion	My vegetable	Reasons	Fanthorpe's vegetable	What's the difference? Which do you prefer?
——— her paleskinned lamps. Rub them for strange knowledge They shine With the light of the tomb	pumpkin	I put pumpkin because you can make lamps out of them, also they have. quite pale skin.	Onions	I would never have put onions. I can see they have a kind of glow about them, possibly you would rub them like Aladdin's lamp, but I think pumpkins is more down to earth.

Think again about the order of things

You have a poem, and you have a picture that goes with it. For example, Fanthorpe's wonderful *Not My Best Side* is based on an Uccello painting of George and the Dragon; Auden's *Musée Des Beaux Arts* refers to various Breughel paintings, notably the one depicting Icarus falling into the sea. Larkin's *An Arundel Tomb* is based on a real tomb in Chichester Cathedral. Reproductions of all such images are easily found on the internet.

So you have two available components in this case: the poem and a picture. A good teacher will teach the poem and show the picture, but a brilliant teacher thinks carefully about how to present these components for maximum effect – including opportunities for *uncontaminated comparison and response*. What's the best sequence for revealing these components?

Not My Best Side

Not my best side, I'm afraid.
The artist didn't give me a chance to
Pose properly, and as you can see,

Poor chap, he had this obsession with
Triangles, so he left off two of my
Feet. I didn't comment at the time
(What, after all, are two feet
To a monster?) but afterwards
I was sorry for the bad publicity.
Why, I said to myself, should my conqueror
Be so ostentatiously beardless, and ride
A horse with a deformed neck and square hoofs?
Why should my victim be so
Unattractive as to be inedible,
And why should she have me literally
On a string? I don't mind dying
Ritually, since I always rise again,
But I should have liked a little more blood
To show they were taking me seriously.

II

It's hard for a girl to be sure if
She wants to be rescued. I mean, I quite
Took to the dragon. It's nice to be
Liked, if you know what I mean. He was
So nicely physical, with his claws
And lovely green skin, and that sexy tail,
And the way he looked at me,
He made me feel he was already to
Eat me. And any girl enjoys that.
So when this boy turned up, wearing machinery,
On a really dangerous horse, to be honest,
I didn't much fancy him. I mean,
What was he like underneath the hardware?
He might have acne, blackheads or even
Bad breath for all I could tell, but the dragon –
Well, you could see all his equipment
At a glance. Still, what could I do?
The dragon got himself beaten by the boy,
And a girl's got to think of her future.

III

I have diplomas in Dragon
Management and Virgin Reclamation.
My horse is the latest model, with
Automatic transmission and built-in
Obsolescence. My spear is custom-built,
And my prototype armour
Still on the secret list. You can't
Do better than me at the moment.
I'm qualified and equipped to the
Eyebrow. So why be difficult?
Don't you want to be killed and/or rescued
in the most contemporary way? Don't
You want to carry out the roles
That sociology and myth have designed for you?
Don't you realise that, by being choosy,
You are endangering job-prospects
In the spear- and horse-building industries?
What, in any case, does it matter what
You want? You're in my way.

A perfectly good lesson can be had by reading how Fanthorpe reacts to Uccello and reworks the Hero–Monster–Damsel archetypes; you read the poem and compare it to the painting. But if you read the poem first, you have lost some key opportunities for comparative response. Fanthorpe's description of the horse's neck is apposite, but if you come to it before you come to the painting, it's not exciting. The painting merely confirms the poem; you cannot react directly to it, nor to the original St George story, if the poem has already kicked in and hijacked your responses. If you can't make your responses first, you cannot fully appreciate the oddness and peculiar accuracy of Fanthorpe's reactions *compared to your own*.

It's necessary to assemble these components to maximum effect. An excellent lesson begins with pupils jotting their own sense of George, the Dragon, and the Maiden, *entirely without seeing the poem or the painting*. They will naturally go to stereotypes. They will assume George to be handsome, the dragon terrifying, the girl beautiful. With these stereotypes in mind, they will then look at the painting, and note any differences from their original thoughts. Often, they will see some differences – the dragon is smaller than they'd thought, and so on – but they won't make the radical responses that Fanthorpe makes. They will, however, begin to see that the stereotypes have been reworked a little.

Only then do they read the poem, which unlocks their responses to the painting, and their reactions are strengthened by their own earlier work, which provides the basis for comparison. They have their original thoughts about the story and its archetypes to compare with Fanthorpe's twentieth-century stereotypes and they can appreciate the comedy and perceptiveness of that journey *because in a sense they have just made it themselves*. Similarly, they can see how comic and impertinent are her responses to the classic painting because *they are more comic and impertinent than their own reactions were*. So a few minutes' thought at the planning stage about the sequence of lesson events can make the difference between competent learning and genuine surprise, discovery, pleasure and understanding.

The gifts of the text

DARTs are useful and objectives essential, but the planning must originate in the text itself. Let the text tell you what to do. Craig Raine's wonderful *A Martian Sends a Postcard Home*, arguably the single most useful classroom poem, sets its own clear agenda of activities. Here is the poem in full.

> Caxtons are mechanical birds with many wings
> and some are treasured for their markings –
>
> they cause the eyes to melt
> or the body to shriek without pain.
>
> I have never seen one fly, but
> sometimes they perch on the hand.
>
> Mist is when the sky is tired of flight
> and rests its soft machine on the ground:
>
> then the world is dim and bookish
> like engravings under tissue paper.
>
> Rain is when the earth is television.
> It has the property of making colours darker.

Model T is a room with the lock inside –
a key is turned to free the world

for movement, so quick there is a film
to watch for anything missed.

But time is tied to the wrist
Or kept in a box, ticking with impatience.

In homes, a haunted apparatus sleeps,
that snores when you pick it up.

If the ghost cries, they carry it
to their lips and soothe it to sleep

with sounds. And yet, they wake it up
deliberately, by tickling with a finger.

Only the young are allowed to suffer
openly. Adults go to a punishment room

with water, but nothing to eat.
They lock the door and suffer the noises

alone. No one is exempt
and everyone's pain has a different smell.

At night, when all the colours die,
they hide in pairs

and read about themselves,
in colour, with their eyes shut.

This poem is a classroom joy, and I regularly use it with 11-year-olds, sixth-formers and postgraduates. It differentiates beautifully: Year 7 see it as riddles, Year 12 can begin to understand from it the idea of the naif narrator (so it's a good starting-point for Atwood's *The Handmaid's Tale* or Brontë's *Wuthering Heights*). It would be madness to impose some sort of external DART on a text like that which offers its own ready-made participation activity of trying to discover what the Martian is actually talking about. Your pupils work in pairs to list the everyday objects and processes that the Martian is describing, and the odd mysteries and beauties of the poetry are discovered. They have to explain their decisions with reference to the text. But even here the learning is stronger when it's held within a clear context. For younger pupils, this may involve continuing the composition of riddles, and reading other mystery poems and stories to gain an understanding of mysterious writing; for sixth-formers this may be a context of understanding essential narrative concepts, such as the non-expert first-person describer; or alternatively it may be an introduction to radical imagery, such as the conceits of John Donne. In all these cases, the poem will not be isolated; and the learning will be consolidated (and evaluated) when the pupils write their own verses showing what the Martian thinks of (for example) eating, posting a letter, televison, school, football. (They read out their verses, and the class has to guess what's being described.)

This lesson cannot fail. I've been grateful to Craig Raine countless times in my teaching career. It implies its own set of activities and generates pleasurable discovery of how writers work, and these are the issues for us in choosing and teaching poems and small texts.

Chapter 5

Managing learning, managing classrooms

The American-Hip-High-School-Teacher enters the classroom for the first time. The disaffected adolescents sneer at him and chew their gum but he is somehow different; he sits for a moment on the edge of the desk, he looks at them with patient humour, he has perhaps a small earring. He writes DEMOCRACY in huge capitals on the board and, intrigued despite themselves, the drug dealers, muggers and amateur prostitutes who make up his first-ever class begin to offer thoughts on DEMOCRACY as it relates to their inner-city lives. Soon, they will give up drug-dealing, mugging and amateur prostitution and form a close-harmony choir which will come second in a prestigious inter-state competition.

This character is as dangerous as he (or she) is charismatic. His agenda is about as wrong as it could be, but his influence is pervasive. He contributes to the miasma of apprehension and misapprehension that surrounds the whole anxious question of making good, working relationships with children. It is an issue that concerns new teachers more than any other.

Of course, your personality is significant here, and you need to think explicitly about your personal strengths and weaknesses; but teaching is a complex and subtle business, not a simple matter of energy, performance and attractiveness. Indeed, a classroom persona built mainly around such qualities is almost certain to fail because it excludes pupils, except as awe-struck audiences. It is certainly true that some teachers seem to have a natural sense of working in a classroom, and some look as though they will never be able to do it; but the majority of us can achieve success with hard work, and *this work lies in preparation more than in performance.*

You should never feel alone in a classroom. Schools have elaborate behaviour policies that only have a chance of working when teachers abandon the maverick-genius approach and work together. Such systems can work surprisingly well. However, they are, for the most part, extrinsic systems, at some distance from teaching and learning. Brilliant teachers use them, but they also recognise that *intrinsic methods, methods that plan good behaviour and good relationships into the classroom work itself, are the best.*

Brilliant class management comes through the work. It recognises that, in the end, high-energy performance is unsustainable and counter-productive, punishments are something of a bluff, and the best rewards lie within English, not in the deployment of a discrete set of "management skills". You want children to work and, if they don't, you have to consider their reasons for not working. They aren't many, or complicated. Children don't work because they can't, or because they don't want to. Good planning (rather then charismatic delivery) makes work accessible, purposeful and enjoyable.

Get the level right

At its most obvious, this concerns the level of academic challenge in the work you're offering. One of the most common planning errors for new teachers is pitching work too high, and this is an area where you should seek advice.

But there's more to it than this. Brilliant teachers differentiate as a matter of habit (see Chapter 10) and differentiated teaching provides a range of access routes to learning. Embedded differentiation isn't about giving out three worksheets (clever, average and not-clever-at-all) but about allowing for different learning styles in your approaches to tasks, instructions and explanations. The machine doesn't start until the penny drops, and the penny drops at different times for different people. It's a simple matter to develop the habit of explaining crucial learning or key instructions in three or four different ways. This needs to be planned in to your lesson.

The shape of the lesson – transitions, and the lesson story

Children are motivated when they see the point (and it's never a bad idea to tell them what the point is, explicitly). You create a sense of purpose and direction by crafting shapely lessons around clear and local objectives. A lesson needs a throughline, a clear story which links the activities to each other and to the learning outcomes. You may need to be quite explicit about these links. Arguably, these links – often manifest as the transition points in the lesson – are the most significant learning moments, moments when the learning becomes explicit. *Good teachers plan activities, but brilliant teachers pay close planning attention to the connections between them.*

We have used various metaphors for lesson planning, such as the lesson as a journey and the plan as the route map, and these all suggest that the lesson is best thought of as a complex event made up of connected parts. The *lesson story* is another helpful planning metaphor. You should be able to say, at least to yourself, and probably to your pupils, "We need to learn the following thing. First of all, we will do activity A. Having done that, we will be able to take a new piece of understanding from it, look at it, and try it in a different way in activity B." *In the moment between the activities, crucial things happen.* The past learning is evaluated and made explicit, and then transferred to the next activity, where it will be extended, modified and developed. If you can't see this link between the two activities, you must modify your planning. If the pupils can't see it, they need to have it pointed out explicitly. But many teachers will simply close the first activity and begin the second.

In Chapter 2 we considered a lesson based on the objective of understanding and enjoying the similes in a poem (Causley's *Timothy Winters*). I watched this lesson recently and recorded the transition moment between the first activity (the creative labelling of similes on a character drawn by the class on the board) and the following one (the reading of the poem, with attention to its similes). Here verbatim is the second part of what the teacher said to her Year 7 class:

Teacher (looking with the class at the images on the whiteboard):

> Well, that's quite a character, isn't it? Quite a fascinating character, we should give him a name, should we? What should we call him? And he's got, what's he got? Spots like ten-penny pieces, apparently. Says Laura. (Laughter). And what's this, hair like grass. Which are, as we are saying, this way of saying it's like something, it gives you a picture, we're saying, it makes you laugh. Ears like toadstools, apparently. (Laughter). We're saying they're called similes, because one thing is similar to the other, when we say it's like something, OK, we're calling that expression a simile. Ears like toadstools is a simile. And the spelling. Say simile, but spell siMILE. SimILE, like MILE. It makes it what, more . . . (Pupil: Funny). Yes, more funny. And perhaps more vivid. A picture in the writing.
>
> And now we're going to have a look at another character, and you'll see he has some similes too. Look for his ears. Not toadstools. Also his teeth. He's called Timothy. (Distributes poem.)

In transcript this may appear laboured, even patronising, but the teacher has recognised that this transition moment is a key moment where the learning becomes explicit, where the objective rises to the surface for focused discussion, and where the next activity is deliberately connected to the last one. Children can see what is being carried across. The throughline, based on the objective, is revealed.

If activities are the bricks of the lesson, transitions are the mortar; and the wall falls down without the mortar.

The lesson beginning: the tumbleweed experience

There's nothing worse, nothing harder to recover from, than a weak beginning. You walk in, you ask your killer question, and the class just looks at you. You ask it again; a note of pleading enters your voice. The silence prospers; tumbleweed is about to blow listlessly across the room. I've died this death many times and the sense of apathy, of non-cooperation, is almost irresistible. Twenty minutes into the lesson you'll have enough momentum to get you out of a hole, but the first three minutes are vital, and you must *plan certain success into your lesson opening.*

It's easy to do. Consider this checklist for your first three minutes

- Start once, not two or three times. If you have to wait a minute, wait, and start cleanly.
- Deal straight away with the whole group, not with individuals who want to talk to you.
- They should all be required to work within three minutes. Work here doesn't necessarily mean write, but it means more than listening to you. Mark this moment on your lesson plan – *when does everyone (not just volunteers) have to work?* I have watched lesson after lesson where no one who doesn't want to is required to actually do anything (other than appear to be listening to the teacher) for twenty minutes or more. Of course, this is a serious learning issue, but it is also a management issue. Children with nothing to do will eventually misbehave. This can happen right in the middle of what appears to be a highly interactive starter if the only contributors are actually volunteers.
- Work from your powerbase – centre front.
- Plan the foothills. Here's another metaphor – if the lesson is a mountain, the opening is the foothills. Everyone must step onto the foothills, and everyone can, because they are seductively gentle and almost flat. You are coaxing an animal out of a cage. For example, begin concrete, not abstract. An opening question like, "Why do we dream?" is likely to bewilder the class, but, "What did you dream about last night?" is likely to provoke some answers. Start with concrete, anecdotal questions which address the pupils' own experiences. "What was the last argument in your house about?" will get you started; "Why do families argue?" may only induce the tumbleweed response. (Could you answer that question out of the blue? *Are you testing your opening questions on a willing friend or lover?*)
- It's good to start with speaking and listening (and you should always try to avoid the temptation to use writing as a management weapon). But don't just ask a question and expect an answer. Allow a minute or two (literally – time it with your watch) of silent jotting first. Now everyone can speak, because they have written something down; you aren't left dependent on volunteers, and no-one can opt out if asked, because you can say, "Just tell us what you've written down . . ."

Task-setting – always QDO

A management blackspot is the time immediately after task-setting when, instead of standing at the centre-front and settling the whole class, the teacher finds herself dealing with a forest of individual enquiries. Children need a considerable amount of conceptual and practical information from you before they can begin something. In one day I recorded the following questions asked immediately after task-setting. Each is a perfectly reasonable question, and each is quite sufficient to prevent a pupil from getting started.

- Is it in the back of our books?
- Do you mean, a real person, or a made-up person?
- How long does it need to be?
- Is it based on the book or is it a new story?
- Does it have to rhyme?
- Is it set out like a playscript?
- How do you set out a playscript?
- Should I finish this other work first?
- Is this for coursework?
- Can we work in pairs?
- Which page is that on?
- Is it a happy or a sad ending?
- Is it a formal letter?
- Where do you put the address?

and so on. There are dozens more of these questions, and a good teacher tries to head them off with clear and full task setting, but it's impossible to anticipate them all. A brilliant teacher uses a routine such as QDO to solve problems with the whole class.

QDO stands for Questions, Deadline and Outcome. Pupils beginning a task should be able to ask about things they don't understand, know how long they've got, and know what's going to happen at the far end. This is embarrassingly obvious but parts of it are frequently omitted. Its regular use can have unexpectedly dramatic results in settling children to work.

Q reminds you to ask if children understand the task, if they have any questions. Of course, children will frequently assert that they do understand, that they don't have any questions; and when you tell them to start, they will put their hands up and start asking. This just seems to be a trade-union rule for pupils – never own up to not understanding. So there are better ways of handling *Q*; for example, why not have pupils always discuss a new task in pairs, for thirty seconds, and decide if they have any problems? Then they can raise their hands and ask. This is now a part of the task-setting; no one has begun, everyone is listening, problems are being raised and solved for everybody. And then you can say to the class, "Is there now anything that will stop you working when I stop talking?"

D reminds you that pupils need to know how long they've got. This allows them to plan the work, obviously; it also provides them with an immediate sense of what you're looking for in terms of depth and detail. And of course deadlines are highly motivating. I am working hard now on this manuscript because my deadline is looming. So use your watch a lot in the lesson; deadlines generate creative energy, and they aren't restricting. You don't have to keep to them, after all.

O is the part of QDO that is often left out. You check that children have no further questions, you tell them how long they've got; you should also tell them where the work is going. Outcome here doesn't mean learning outcome or objective; it means what will happen next. The outcome from a piece of planning might be a GCSE coursework assignment; the outcome from silent poetry writing might be a class reading; the outcome from group discussion might be a feedback to the whole class. Teachers will almost always plan the outcome, but it's surprising how rarely children are informed about it at the outset. Starting off to discuss fox-hunting may engage you. Starting off to discuss fox-hunting knowing that you've got to reach a conclusion in twenty minutes is more engaging. Starting off to discuss fox-hunting knowing that in twenty minutes you're going to have to discuss your conclusions with the whole class is even more motivating.

Talking to the class – using questions

Teachers rightly love questions. If I write *How tall is Prince Phillip?* you cannot help, momentarily, picturing him and thinking about an answer. Questions are difficult to resist. All teachers know that there are different sorts of questions – open, closed, convergent, divergent, factual, rhetorical, opinion-based, and so on; and using a range is a good thing. Children like the security of right answers just as much as they like the freedom of exploration and opinion. What matters most is that *they understand what sort of question is being asked.*

This involves the teacher in being open and straightforward about it. You ask a good question, but do you also say, "There's no right answer to this question"? More to the point, do you sometimes say, "This question *does* have a right answer"? Children don't mind, but they like to know. The least motivating process, but one I see frequently, is where the teacher asks closed questions as if they were open ones. She has asked for an opinion about the effect of a piece of text. For example, she has asked pupils for their reactions to the use of short sentences in a paragraph of prose fiction. *Although she has asked for opinions, she really has one clear answer in mind –* that the short sentences create suspense. As she takes answers from volunteers, she grazes the class until the right answer is offered. One pupil suggests that short sentences make the writing seem childish; another offers the view that the short sentences make the writing more descriptive; a third thinks that they are quite annoying. I have heard myself doing this so many times. To these pupils I say, "Ye-es . . . ?" in a sort of rising diphthong, which anyone can tell actually means, "Yes, but . . . ?" – or, in fact, "No!" The children know by now that *they are not being asked for their opinions at all; they are being asked to guess the teacher's opinion.* When someone finally works out that this concerns suspense, the excited "Yes!" that rewards the pupil is fundamentally different to the earlier responses.

I have sat in many lessons watching this process, and I watch the reactions of pupils who have offered a perfectly good answer to the question. They have been asked for a relevant opinion and have volunteered one, only to be snubbed. Their expressions at these moments are revealing. The mood is one of subliminal irritation. If you don't value my opinion, don't pretend that you do. I'll think twice before I volunteer again.

Valuing and validating pupil responses

In fact, this whole area of listening to pupils is seriously important in building good classroom atmosphere. Consider the child who volunteers any kind of contribution. He is making a genuine and quite possibly a difficult commitment to you. There may be all kinds of peer pressure against putting his hand up. *You absolutely must reward this commitment.*

All teachers listen to pupils but the validating of pupil contributions needs to be explicit. Contributions to discussion are validated when their *content* is addressed. Often, the contribution is rewarded with praise, and this is helpful; the teacher says "Good!" or "Well done!" and moves on to the next answer. It's better then nothing, but a string of "goods" punctuating a class discussion doesn't motivate at a high level. What motivates is the teacher actually taking the time (a few seconds, probably, no more) to discuss what the pupil has said. When this happens – the teacher asks a question back to the pupil, clarifying and developing a point in the pupil's argument – not only is the learning being progressed, but the balance of relationship in the room is moving towards genuine conversation. "Good!" is merely assessive; the teacher remains entirely in charge of knowledge and opinion, and so shouldn't be surprised if pupils seem reluctant to join in.

The use of the whiteboard as a repository of pupil ideas – a list of one-word reminders of what pupils have said – is a simple but highly motivating tool. The pupils' ideas are published; they remain powerful for a few minutes, rather than disappearing into thin air; there is a symbolism about their words appearing in the teacher's work space.

In all of these matters of running a classroom, what we are seeing is that good learning and good behaviour go together. In the end, if pupils aren't motivated by the work, they won't be motivated by anything. With especially difficult classes, this can be a long, slow process, requiring frequent re-working and compromise to bring your agenda closer to that of the pupils. It won't happen on the first day, even if you do wear an earring and odd socks.

Don't YAVA

We have said that pupils need to be required to work, though this work may not be writing; it may be answering teacher's questions. I have often watched teachers YAVA for twenty minutes at a time; but YAVA requires nothing of non-volunteers. YAVA stands for *You Ask, Volunteers Answer*: hands go up, keen volunteers speak; the lesson can feel very lively; the teacher will often think that things went rather well. For a couple of minutes, this is an active thing to do; but it has a very limited life. If you're not volunteering, you know that no one is going to bother you. The keen participants at the front can do the work; all you've got to do is keep quiet and avoid the teacher's eye. Don't you remember doing that at school? I spent two years in chemistry staring at the grain on the desk while my fresh-faced chemistry mates rattled on with Mr Webster about molecules and compounds. Everybody was happy, including me.

This is a major learning issue and, as so often, it's also a management issue. One person opting out is a problem; in the YAVA classroom, typically one-third of the pupils are participating. A majority doing nothing is a management timebomb.

So don't YAVA, even though you will see experienced teachers doing it all the time. Of course you must ask questions; of course you must reward volunteers by taking their answers and engaging with them; but consider the fundamental change in the mood of the room when you ask just one non-volunteer to answer (and remember that previous jotting will help). This isn't only a change for the one person you ask; it's a change for all the non-combatants in the room, who suddenly realise that they may be next, so they'd better start thinking and listening. Don't abandon your volunteers; but mix them with non-volunteers always when talking to the whole class.

Managing speaking and listening

People talk more than they read or write, so speaking and listening must be a major part of your English lessons. A teacher asked me recently why his Year 8 behaved so badly. We looked at his medium-term planning; no speaking and listening for five weeks. Children will talk; your best hope is to make the talk legitimate rather than subversive. So speaking and listening are your management allies. If you're inclined to the opposite view – that oral work is likely to cause bad behaviour, and so best avoided with difficult classes – you're in danger of initiating a vicious circle. Nailing them down to silent writing may be a short-term fix but is simply storing up negative pressure in the medium term. Anyway, speaking and listening are central to English learning, to the National Curriculum, and to the Literacy Framework.

There is no magic in the management of speaking and listening. It requires what all good English requires – careful planning, clear objectives, thoughtful structures, clear focus. Behaviour is managed by the lesson plan.

Let's consider, for example, the management of group discussion. What are the management danger points? Children may not talk; some may dominate to the detriment of others in the group; they may talk about *EastEnders*; they may make too much noise; you may not be able to properly monitor or control the discussion. Setting aside the point that any good teacher takes risks from time to time, we can easily deal with these danger points by good planning.

Is the work integrated?

Try not to set up wholly separate oral activities. You may need to create formal presentations, perhaps for assessment purposes, but you can probably assess speaking and listening in a number of environments; indeed, you are probably required to. The best group discussions connect with other work. They may be about texts, for example, or they may reflect text-type analysis work. If you're looking at estate agents' language, why not try selling the classroom? If you're considering the language of journalism, why not set up three-minute news bulletins based on pupils' own news stories? (This work is outlined in Chapter 7.) These are examples of how speaking and listening work connects to other work. This doesn't, however, mean that all speaking and listening should lead to formal presentation, or to a written outcome. It does mean that the class is warmed up to the discussion.

Are you thinking about the formation of the group?

Four people is enough. Larger groups split or isolate individuals. Varying grouping is essential – friendship groups, mixed-gender groups, extrovert/introvert mixes, random groups where you just meet somebody new to work with.

Are you helping with the internal working of the group?

Groups are so often given a topic and left to it. Here as ever you have to plan from the pupils' viewpoint. Will they be able simply to get on with it? Do you need to advise them how to proceed? Do they need to define their group roles, such as group leader, group note-maker, group arguer?

This last is a brilliant addition to group work. One member is appointed devil's advocate (though you might not use the phrase). His job is to listen to the arguments and counter them. This is fun but also creates a whole new dynamic in the discussions. You can create other generic roles as well – such as a group pacifier, a group problem-solver. It is worth taking time over the definition of these roles. For example, the group note-maker is more than just a dogsbody; it is her job to pause the discussion from time to time to recap and agree

Table 5.1 Group roles

Leader	Ensure that everyone gets a turn. Ensure that everyone listens. Ensure that the discussion brief is covered. Watch the time.
Note-maker	Record the discussion. Pause the discussion from time to time and summarise it with the group, checking your understanding. Contribute to feedback.
Arguer	Listen to and challenge arguments and opinions. Ask others to justify their arguments. Offer counter-arguments, especially if the discussion is quiet.
Pacifier	Help leader and members to reconcile opposing views. Offer compromises. Discuss changes of view among members.
Member	Offer views and evidence for them. Listen to other views, possibly making notes. Modify your views if appropriate.
Feedback organiser	Work with leader, note-maker and all group members to organise feedback. Check feedback requirements. Keep appropriate notes. Remind leader and group of timing so that feedback can be addressed.

on the positions reached so far. The leader does more than simply keeping it going; for example, she must ensure that everybody speaks and is heard. Brilliant teachers spend time on these roles, preferably by creating role cards for all members of the group that define their responsibilities. Even members with no additional job have a role card that defines the whole business of offering views, offering evidence, listening to counter-arguments, considering how to respond, moving towards compromise, and so on.

It may take you an hour to make a set of group-discussion role cards like this, but you can use them over and over again and your pupils will become used to them and need them less and less.

Are they preparing for the discussion?

They can prepare by making relevant notes that they bring to the discussion so they all have a flying start. Think about useful structures for this. A simple continuum – a line with *totally in favour of fox-hunting* at one end and *totally against fox-hunting* at the other, with a mid-point ready marked – will allow pupils to focus on where they stand. They put their personal marks on the line and write a few sentences explaining their decision; they arrive at the group discussion with this information already in place.

Are you structuring the discussion?

Pupils need clear structure. You need to break down the discussion into timed components such as ten minutes for opening comments, time for main discussion, and so on. But you also need to structure the content. The discussion may focus on a prompt sheet. The prompt sheet might be:

- a series of questions to answer;
- a series of statements to place in order of preference;
- a series of statements to sort into given columns;
- a series of continua (see above) for group agreement and completion;
- a series of statements (or a single statement) with which to agree or disagree;

and so on.

Do you QDO?

They need to know how long they've got, and they need frequent reminders. They need warning as they approach the end. In particular, they need advance warning of the nature of any feedback. Preparing the feedback to the whole class is a task in itself and they need help with doing this, including a time allocation for it. They can't have a lively discussion and then just cobble together a feedback at the last minute. They need help with its content; they need to think about purpose and audience; they need to practise it.

Are you monitoring the groups?

You will develop a sense of when groups are flagging and need your subtle and brief intervention. It's easy to tell whether a group has strayed off the point and often all you need to do is to go and stand near it. You need to combine your accessibility to the groups with your visibility to the whole class. Often, teachers set pupils off on activities and then plunge into the body of the room, kneeling at tables (which is a good thing) while the behaviour in the room drops as the noise levels rise. This can go on for twenty minutes and things get steadily worse because the teacher has effectively, almost literally, disappeared. Children need periodic sight of you to remember where they are and what the background structures are. Don't circle from group to group – for one thing, this makes your path predictable. Visit a group, then return to the centre-front and stay there; you don't have to speak, or do teacher-glaring; just be visible; then visit another group.

Of course, pupils will digress; they will talk about football and boyfriends, you have to accept this, just as you have to accept that their minds will wander when they're sitting in silence. Of course, when they're talking, at least you know what they're talking about!

Stirring the tea

You are the spoon in the teacup. If you want to stir the class up, you must move around. At that danger moment of starting up group or pair discussions, when you're wondering if they might just sit there self-consciously not saying anything (a tumbleweed moment) you need to get away from the centre-front, start moving around. The noise will start. But when you need them to quieten down, stop stirring; stand still. I've seen so many teachers stirring the class up by walking around, kneeling, disappearing, while periodically nagging them to be quiet. You can't expect both: you can't stir the tea and expect it to remain stationary.

Listening

The groups have finished their discussions and prepared their feedbacks. Now each group will speak. In management terms, this is another blackspot. Children aren't especially good at listening to each other. Telling them to listen because it's polite to listen has limited power; children spend a lot of time doing things that aren't polite. Expecting them to listen out of genuine interest is optimistic. For one thing, listening to six feedbacks about fox-hunting is tedious, even if they're good. And it gets worse as the same points are repeated. Groups waiting their turn are likely to be more preoccupied with whispered preparation than with listening. Groups who have already performed are demob-happy. So how do we manage the listening?

For one thing, we vary the nature of feedbacks. We don't always have them; the value of the work is in the discussion process, not the feedback product. Or we only take feedbacks from some of the groups. Or we move randomly around the room. Or we have different feedback methods – my favourite is the envoy, where the single feedback-giver from each group moves around the groups, reporting to each one, discussing the issues, and then moving on.

And secondly, we focus on the listeners. In any classroom where a child (or, indeed, a teacher) is talking and twenty-five children are listening, *the teacher's attention needs to be focused not on the speaker – he has something to do – but on the listeners.* Give them a reason for listening. Tell them they must make particular notes, or answer or ask particular questions about what they're listening to. I recently had groups designing mobile phone advertisements. I gave them a sheet with a long list of phone features (internet, music, video camera, stock exchange service, coloured cases, etc.) and a list of possible audiences for the product (teenagers, technology lovers, technology haters, and so on). This was their prompt sheet. They discussed and designed a phone advertisement, selecting features for an audience that they'd chosen from my list. The feedback involved them presenting their advertisements to the whole class. However, I asked them not to reveal which of the audiences they'd chosen. We had to listen to their presentations, look at their paper adver- tisements, and guess which audience they were working to. This simple element of game meant that everyone listened very carefully. *Remember: the listeners need a reason to listen.*

Motivating pupils – the element of game

This element of game is strongly motivating in many areas of English. While working on a class reader, for example, you may want to analyse what makes narrative believable. Why do we actually believe that a boy has found an angel in his garage? All kinds of work can centre around this idea. Story games encourage pupils to consider how to make a story convincing. The simplest true or false game leads to discussions of tone, detail, description, reactions of char- acters; this can all be handled orally and then re-applied to a text, or to pupils' own writing. A pupil (or, at the beginning, the teacher) tells the class a story which is neither mundane nor impossible (I tell one about seeing a UFO on Glastonbury). The pupils ask questions and then guess whether it's true or not. There follows a discussion of their verdicts in terms of the convincing or unconvincing narrative features. The *alibi* game is a development of this. A pair of pupils creates a joint story (their "alibi" for some unspecified and irrelevant crime). The first child enters the classroom and is quizzed on the story. The second then does the same; she has not heard the answers of the first child. If their stories match, they have won – their "alibi" stands up. The point of the game is that you win if you have planned your story in sufficient detail. Such games are enormously popular, and they allow you to discuss important text-level features – of their own and others' writing – in a productive and committed atmosphere.

Motivating pupils – joint ownership

You don't want to break a thing if it belongs to you. Children behave better if they have genuine involvement. Opinions, for example, are very motivating; children who frankly don't care why Jane Eyre behaves as she does will nevertheless have quite clear views as to how she *should* behave, and how they would behave in her situation, and these are part of a legitimate reader response.

Negotiation and flexibility are powerful and strengthen your authority if handled correctly. I don't mean weak negotiation (Teacher: *I want you to write an essay about ships.* Pupils: *Do we have to?* Teacher: *Oh, all right then*) but pro-active negotiation where the teacher introduces limited choices; for example, you may allow pupils to choose between written and oral outcomes. Particularly, you should make every effort to involve pupils as experts. Why do they have to discuss fox-hunting if in fact they have strong opinions or knowledge about something else? Let them choose.

Quietness is golden

When children or adults are asked what they value in a teacher they rarely comment on subject knowledge. Instead, they talk about values – enthusiasm, approachability, fairness, organisation. One important value is credibility. They have to believe you. Setting punishments you won't carry out is a sure way of losing credibility. Writing an ever-growing list of detention-names on the board is a credibility trap – are you really going to keep the whole class in? And asking for silence and not meaning it or not getting it is a way of handing control over to the pupils.

Silence is an absolute. Don't use the word as a synonym for quietness. Silence means nobody speaks, at all, for any reason. You may need pupils to be silent, and you can achieve this, so long as you take some trouble over it. You need to

- explain what silence is, literally;
- tell them why it matters, with regard to the particular nature of the work (in terms perhaps of concentration, or privacy, or originality of thought);
- tell them for how long it's going to last – and this must be a short time, perhaps three minutes. Anyone can be silent for three minutes, but no one can seriously set out to be silent for an unspecified time – could you?

- ensure they're all prepared before the silence begins;
- watch them and use low-key control if necessary to maintain the silence.

You shouldn't ask for silence if there isn't a work-related reason for it; if you do require it, you must take some trouble over it. Like most management issues, it has to do with the content of what you're doing, and requires explicit but low-key handling in a collaborative atmosphere. Of course, it's naive to simply assert that appropriate work, well planned, will eradicate uncooperative behaviour; but it's a certainty that inappropriate, poorly planned teaching will guarantee it, so planning must be the first place you go to when improving behaviour management.

Chapter 6

Evaluation

For me, evaluating my teaching used to be a subjective business. As the children left the room, I would say, "Well, I think that went rather well!" or, "Well, they seemed to enjoy it . . ." If I had taught something, quite well in my opinion, to an apparently interested class, then my assumption was that they had learned it. This is still a common equation: *decent teaching plus reasonably co-operative class equals learning.* When asking a question such as, "Why are you sure they all understand speech marks?" I frequently receive the answer, "Because we did them last week."

But I did used to notice discontinuities – for example, the disappointing discrepancy between what seemed to be a lively lesson and a poor written follow-up. Concepts were explained, discussed and illuminated in the lesson, perhaps largely orally (and perhaps with excess YAVA); but later in the week, when I read the resulting writing, I would be surprised to find that understanding was far from secure. This has happened to me many times. I am swayed by an active and cheerful speaking-and-listening session into a subjective, implicit but wayward evaluation of the learning, and this is only corrected days later. Of course your impression of the lesson is important, but your evaluation can't stop there. Evaluation needs to be swifter, more objective, and more explicit than that.

You need to evaluate your own work for two essential and connected purposes – to improve pupil learning, and to improve your own practice. If pupils aren't learning, you need to consider very quickly how to modify your approaches. When things go well, you need to clarify the success for yourself so that you can build on it both in terms of their immediate learning and your continuing development.

Brilliant teachers are evaluating pretty well all of the time, and if this seems a daunting prospect, here are two reassurances. Firstly, you are almost certainly doing a lot more evaluation than you think; and secondly, it's possible to rationalise evaluation into a straightforward and highly manageable component of lesson planning.

What evaluation isn't

Let's continue to clarify what good evaluation isn't. We've said that it shouldn't be purely impressionistic. Neither is evaluation an afterthought: it is *an essential component of your planning, built into your lesson before you teach it.*

Similarly, evaluation isn't a complete sweep of every possible lesson issue; it needs to be focused. If allowed to run out of control, it attempts to cover everything – the children's entry into the room, how quickly they settled, whether the weather affected them, whether it was Friday afternoon, how well they responded to questioning, whether they were silent when asked, how much help they needed with the tasks, how noisy they were, whether you talked too much, how well you explained things, how your pace and timing went, how effectively you prepared and used resources . . . The problem with such diffuse and ambitious evaluation is that it can obscure the only question that really matters. *Did they achieve the learning objectives?* All other questions are subsidiaries.

Evaluation isn't a synonym for assessment; in a sense, evaluation is about your work rather than theirs. Naturally, however, the formal and informal assessment of pupils' work provides a major indicator of how well you're doing, as well as being a significant driver of the curriculum. (English teachers have a huge marking workload, which they discharge admirably, and brilliant teachers always remember why we mark. *We mark to keep the bargain* – pupils work for us; we should work for them. *We mark to provide an audience* – so we should always try to engage with the content of pupils' writing, not simply write an assessive comment. The best written comments I've seen extend the writing by asking questions about it, which the pupil may answer – a written dialogue develops around the pupil's work. *We mark to diagnose and begin to correct errors* – so our error correction needs to be focused around clear patterns, reflecting pupil need or current teaching objectives for the class. (There is, of course, no point in correcting all errors. It might make us feel better, but provides no focus or continuity for pupil learning.) *We mark to celebrate pupil talents and successes on which we can build. We mark to gather information about the pupil*, which we may need to publish to other people. But most importantly, *we mark and assess in order to improve the pupils' learning*. We can't plan the journey without a sense of the starting point.

The information that marking and assessment provide naturally helps us to evaluate the effectiveness of our teaching; but it can be a cumbersome process, and we need to evaluate on a short timescale as well. We need to plan the next lesson, or the next stage of the lesson, or the next sentence of our explanation, in the light of how things are going. At least, we need to evaluate the learning before the lesson ends, so that we can modify our plans for tomorrow.

What evaluation is

At its simplest, evaluation is asking and answering three questions as your pupils leave the classroom:

*   What were they meant to learn?
*   Did they learn it?
*   How do I know?

Earlier chapters on the centrality of learning objectives (especially Chapters 2 and 3) dealt with the first of these; and one of the advantages of working always to clear and specific objectives is that you have a basis for answering the other two questions, and this is your basis for evaluation.

Three levels of evaluation

It helps to think of evaluation as happening at three levels. At a minimum level, you need to evaluate learning at the end of each lesson. At another level, it is a permanent feature of your teaching. There is a middle way between these that is highly effective and might be a good place to begin creating a semi-formal evaluation practice.

The middle level – evaluating activities

As we said in Chapter 5, the lesson has a progressive narrative. The first activity creates a piece of understanding that, at the transition point, will be discussed explicitly and then developed into a second activity. The transition point, as we've said, is a crucial learning moment. It's also a crucial moment of evaluation.

So you might establish a habit of evaluating learning at each transition point – after each activity. I recently watched a lesson with a middle-ability Year 10 group which was about pre-twentieth-century short stories (a common GCSE component and a familiar interpretation of Key Stage 4 requirements). The teacher wanted to explain that stories reflect the culture in which they're written. She began by explaining what she meant by culture – listening to this was the pupils' first activity. They then had to match statements about nineteenth-century culture (the rise of science at the expense of religion, for example; or an increasing interest in the paranormal) against the plots of three or four stories, which they'd previously read.

This matching exercise was well prepared and potentially very effective, but the pupils struggled with it. It became clear that many of them were confused by the initial definition of culture, which was essential for the second activity to work. *The first activity (pupil listening) had not been evaluated – their understanding had not been checked and was in fact far short of the teacher's assumptions.* Had the first activity been more interactive, evaluation would have presented itself by default; but, in the event, the teacher needed to be sure that the pupils understood, but had planned no method of finding out. A potentially excellent and well-planned lesson failed because of this.

So our structure should be based on explicit evaluation at the end of each activity. We need to know now whether the pupils have any sense of what we mean by culture, or euphemism, or dramatic irony, or the active and passive voice. We can't go on to our next activity without being sure of this, and we can't just assume that they've learned it because we've taught it.

How does activity-level evaluation happen?

For this straightforward system of evaluating each activity we need to plan the evaluative mechanism; this is part of your lesson plan, which now has three key components – *learning objective, activity and evaluation.*

So you sketch out in your plan the closing activity, which will evaluate the learning. This will be a brief activity, joined more or less seamlessly to the learning activity, or integrated within it. As well as providing you with a snapshot of the learning up to that point, it will enable the pupils to sustain and consolidate that learning for themselves. Of course the simplest method is to ask children if they understand, but this has limited value. Children usually say they understand, even when they don't; they frankly prefer bewilderment to a repetition of the explanation. (This reminds me of asking for directions when lost in the car. A helpful local gives accurate but complicated directions through the window. After the third turn to the left past the pub I'm completely lost. Why do I keep on pretending I'm following him? Why do I finally say I've got it when I'm nowhere near it?) So try some slightly more elaborate methods.

- They could discuss in pairs a key question about the learning, and then feed back their answers.
- They could give their own created examples – for example, their own euphemisms or their own riddles.
- They could create a one-sentence explanation for other pupils in other classes.
- They could write three key words on their whiteboards.
- They could design their own evaluative questions.
- They could restate the learning objectives in new words.

- They could suggest what the next objective might be.
- They could provide a real-world example of dramatic irony.
- They could explain how this activity related to earlier ones in previous lessons.

Permanent evaluation

You are probably doing a good deal of this already. It doesn't replace the need for more formal evaluation after each activity or, at least, at the end of each lesson. It does require you to be highly sensitive as you monitor reactions in the room.

Almost any classroom activity provides evaluative information and brilliant teachers are permanently susceptible to this. From the first moment of any lesson, you are bombarded with evaluative input. This isn't especially scientific or even systematic; for example, it doesn't always evaluate the learning of every individual; but it's immensely valuable in steering the work. When children are reading aloud, you are checking whether they're understanding what they're reading and reflecting on the appropriateness of the text (this can be very revealing with Shakespeare). When you question the class, you have immediate insight from the nature and frequency of their answers into the appropriateness of the level of work and your explanations so far. Their questions to you signal their comfort level. For example, when you set a task and ask for questions (QDO) and you are faced with a large number of them, you know immediately that your explanation has been unclear and you should stop and re-present it to the whole group. When they're discussing in pairs, you are listening to snippets of discussion; when they're writing, you're looking over their shoulders. When they're feeding back, you're checking their understanding; when they're collaborating with you in a piece of shared writing, you're aware of whether they get the points about the nature of what you're doing. When you're talking to the whole class, you're looking at their faces. The more interactive your teaching becomes, the more frequent and immediate is the evaluation. Literacy *Framework* starters, for example, model teaching which provides evaluative data minute-by-minute. You aren't just estimating whether they're getting it right; you're estimating whether the teaching is doing its job, is accurately pitched and effectively carried out.

The plenary for end-of-lesson evaluation

The literacy *Framework* (see Chapter 7) recognises the value of a final lesson activity that consolidates and evaluates the learning. This is a highly significant and effective component of the *Framework* lesson, though it is often neglected. Books of starters have been published, but the plenary suffers by comparison. New teachers, for one thing, struggle with timing for two reasons – because it's difficult to estimate how long things will take, and because it's difficult to depart from the lesson script in the middle of a lesson which is clearly over-running. This is a problem that vanishes with experience, but it often leaves in its wake a poor habit of lesson finishing. The plenary quite often disappears in practice; or it is relegated to setting home-work and packing up, or to a quick "What did we learn today?" session, on the bell, the pupils already standing up to leave. At this point, they'll say anything to get out of the room. If the objectives are obvious to them, they'll say they understand them. This is quite possibly meaningless.

Your hour lesson needs a ten-minute plenary (not a five-minute one) and this needs to be a planned activity that will enable you to gauge the mood of the room in terms of your learning objectives, to have a sense at least of the majority achievement, and to consider modifications for tomorrow. Routine is good here, but so is variety; so your plenary activity could be chosen from a list such as this:

- I didn't tell you today's objectives – now, what do you think they were?
- Explain today's learning in one sentence to a specified audience such as your mum, a seven-year-old child, a class in the year below yours.
- In pairs – what was the most important thing *in your opinion* that you learned today?
- Sum up today's learning in exactly fifteen words.
- In pairs, think up a new (better?) activity to teach today's objective.
- Write an advertisement or a film trailer for today's lesson.
- Write a two-minute radio news story summing up what happened in today's lesson.
- That's the objective – but tell me one other thing you learned today.
- Look back at today's activities – what was the connection?

- Write a newspaper headline for today's lesson.
- Write one more example of your own.
- As a class, complete two columns on the whiteboard headed CLEAR and NOT CLEAR about what we've learned and what still confuses us.
- Write one thing from today that needs more explanation.
- What do you guess the next lesson will be about, and why?
- What does the next lesson *need* to be about?

Even suggestions beginning *Write* here are predominantly speaking and listening suggestions. You will emphasise speed here; you will glance at the jottings; you will listen to as many contributions as possible – evaluative plenaries are swift and interactive.

(And then later, if an observer says, "I don't think they understood what you were saying about compound sentences," and you reply, "Well, I think they did!" , and he says, "Well, how do you know?" you can point to your plenary evaluation and win the argument.)

Some of the later suggestions on this list suggest how a sustained habit of evaluation through plenaries and elsewhere can generate a truly collaborative classroom ethos. Pupils are being invited to drive the learning forward explicitly by considering where it needs to go next. They are participating in evaluation not so much of their own work or of the teacher's efforts but of the learning as a joint operation. The following lesson can in a sense be jointly planned, or at least modified. The teacher can offer her proposed alternatives for tomorrow's lesson and invite comment. The responsibility for the learning is being shared.

This doesn't mean, obviously, that the final responsibility isn't yours. If learning isn't secure, or behaviour is not as it should be, you have to consider what you can do about your own practice to improve things rather than simply blaming children for misbehaving or not listening carefully. Evaluation should provoke two levels of activity for you. In the short (or immediate) term, it might lead you to change the work currently underway with a specific class. In the longer term, it should help you with forward planning and your own development. Table 6.1 shows some judgments and consequent actions that I noted trainee teachers taking over a period of a few weeks.

In these cases we see teachers using various levels of input to evaluate their work, making immediate modification if necessary and considering their own development. While written outcomes

Table 6.1 Using evaluations

Input	Evaluation	Short-term action	Long-term action
Children reading Shakespeare aloud badly – stumbling, etc.	Text more challenging than I'd thought; lower understanding than anticipated	More text editing, more active approaches, more checking of learning	More care over text choices; more forward planning re: editing; more DARTs; more checking of understanding
Nearly half the class had questions after task-setting	Explanation not as detailed as it needed to be; no QDO	Stopped class, went through instructions more carefully; QDO	Plan instructions, task-setting more elaborately; anticipate pupil problems; test instructions on husband; write out instruction script for self
Main activity newspaper articles were mostly written without journalism language	Inadequate text-type analysis in starter; too many ideas too quickly, starter inadequately evaluated	Stopped activity and looked again at newspaper cuttings, drawing attention to examples of stock vocabulary and phrases	Use full prompt script for starter; spend more time on key concepts; check learning, don't over-estimate; more focus in planning, use examples rather than blanket coverage
Children over-excited and noisy in drama	Lack of focus in group work; lack of theatre discipline	Stopped group work and explained deadlines, audience's need to understand their pieces	Much more pro-active regarding the essential discipline of drama; establish routines for control and some ground rules; provide much more structure for group work; QDO
Disappointing feedbacks after good group discussions	Not enough time and structure given specifically for the feedbacks	Stopped after two feedbacks and encouraged all groups to spend ten more minutes on them	Vary feedbacks; sometimes, no feedback at all; treat feedback as separate task needing its own structure and time
Children inattentive during reading of class reader	Children were bored by novel	Stopped reading after fifteen minutes	Think carefully about choice of texts; vary reading strategies and voices; use shorter reading periods; give

Table 6.1 continued

			focus questions before the reading; QDO (especially O) before reading
Plenary shows continuing confusion between simile and metaphor	Teaching the two together has compounded the confusion!	Re-defined metaphor, did another separation activity	Don't teach pairs like this! Teach either simile or metaphor in an appropriate context

certainly provide rich evaluative material, the more immediate evaluations happen in active and interactive lessons. The more pupil involvement, the more obvious the evaluation. This can be formalised into whole systems of pupil evaluation, where pupils evaluate each other's work and their own. Pupils certainly benefit from systematic evaluation of their own work and brilliant teachers invite this through regular discussion and by encouraging pupils to reflect, perhaps in writing, as a matter of course. Pupil logs can contain progressive personal accounts of developments, problems solved, talents fostered, preferences discovered. As well as benefiting pupils, such logs support English teachers in the continuing task of evaluating and improving their own work.

Chapter 7

The *Framework*

Key issues

The *Framework for Teaching English in Years 7, 8 and 9* is now firmly in charge. It is huge, supported by extensive training and lorry-loads of materials, and it would be pointless to summarise it here. It is however timely to take stock of it and consider its key issues as they support our development as English teachers.

Explicitness

The *Framework* centres on explicitness – in the analysis of text, in the understanding of purpose and audience, in the teaching of grammar. This means that we can make more reliable assumptions about the literacy of our pupils than we used to. We can intervene more effectively in their language, assuming a common and explicit vocabulary; we can say, "I like the way you've used onomatopoeia there", or "Did you mean to use a singular verb there with a plural pronoun?" without having to spiral off into a mini-grammar defining all of the points with reference to other points, none of which is understood – an awful, hole-digging, eye-glazing exercise with a virtual guarantee of failure. Any strategy that gets rid of that gets my vote.

This is certainly happening, even in Year 7, when teachers have some sense of what the Literacy Strategy has been doing with their new pupils. Of course, wrong assumptions are worse than no assumptions at all, and the progression in reality is far from universal. The reconciliation of consistency with teacher- and learner-individuality will always be a work in progress and so issues such as the transitions between schools and key stages remain a focus of activity. Nevertheless, the *Framework* and the Key Stage 3 Strategy of which it's a part, together with the National Literacy Strategy, are remarkable in their resourcing and their achievement of something closer to consistency than we've ever seen before. The centrality of explicitness is a real step forward in classroom practice.

Of course there's a cost. I heard a primary school head say recently, "They know what a subordinate clause is. But they haven't painted a picture for three months." So clearly we must consider a balanced approach to the *Framework*. For example, it has never postulated a literacy hour for secondary pupils, and, while it offers an excellent framework for progression, the lesson shape which it does advocate – the three- or four-part lesson – isn't mandatory.

Objectives

The *Framework* puts learning objectives at the heart of teaching (see Chapter 3) and this is highly beneficial, a direct line to brilliant teaching. *Framework* lessons are based on clarity of outcomes, explicit sharing of objectives, focused planning (see Chapter 2) and secure evaluation (see Chapter 6). This is a remarkable sea-change in English teaching, which for two or three decades had placed activities at the centre.

Framework objectives provide a spinal cord for planning and development, but we must adopt and adapt them with care. The choice of objectives in the long term is a crucial matter of school policy, and then the interpretation of those objectives is essential to individual short term and lesson planning. A productive approach is to take the *Framework* objective from the medium- or short-term plan, *match it with other relevant objectives*, and rewrite them in terms of the lesson and the class. This supplemental rewriting concerns the immediate needs of the class and the resources available as well as the requirements of the medium-term plan (see Chapter 3).

Thus, you may be reading a class novel with Year 7 and want to draw attention to a feature of its construction, which is that a writer may use varying sentence lengths and types to add pace and variety to his writing. This is referred to in the *Framework* as a sentence-level objective; pupils will learn to

> vary the structure of sentences within paragraphs to lend pace, variety and emphasis

and it also appears at text-level (Reading), where pupils will learn to

> recognise how writers' language choices can enhance meaning, e.g. repetition, emotive vocabulary, varied sentence structure or line length, sound effects

It's a good idea to *connect these objectives* in your practice because this reflects the synergy of analytical and creative work (see Chapter 2). So finding matching objectives in different parts of the *Framework* will help you to plan holistically and with differentiation (see Chapter 10).

You then need to rewrite the objective in local terms, such as

> pupils will recognise how Almond uses a variety of sentences to create contrasting moods (at the beginning of Chapter Two) and how they can use this idea in their own new-school stories.

While celebrating this movement to objectives we should be wary of the dead hand of objectives-bureaucracy on our lessons. I've watched many a lesson (and attended many a training event) which began by presenting the objectives on a whiteboard or *PowerPoint* screen, proceeded to work through them, then returned to confirm that they'd been met. After an hour or a day you seem to have travelled nowhere, or rather gone round in a slow circle and returned to your starting point. Sharing objectives is normally a good thing, but it needs to be done with a subtlety that allows lessons to be places of growth and discovery.

For example, I've recently seen very effective, *Framework*-derived teaching where the objectives are partly but not wholly revealed at the beginning. You may in effect be saying:

> We will look at how the writer uses emotion and relationship to prepare us for the ending of the book. We'll look at one or two other features of the ending as well.

And then in your plenary, you would be saying:

> Well, we looked at emotion and relationship. What else did the author do to prepare us for the book's ending?

And of course it's perfectly legitimate to keep the objectives to yourself occasionally, if you've a reason for doing so.

The lesson shape

The three- or four-part lesson isn't a straitjacket but it's a simple, progressive structure that promotes variety.

The *starter* has received a lot of attention. It's remarkable for, amongst other things, single-handedly convincing an entire generation of sceptical teachers to start teaching explicit grammar. The idea of close, highly interactive focus on specific issues which are then realised and contextualised in subsequent work is a dynamic one, offering a paccy solution to the ancient problem of *relating the general to the specific in English teaching*.

In fact it's in these relationships that the starter has most to offer, and this raises the question of how the starter should be used within the overall shape and direction of the lessons. There are two main approaches to this: the *vertical* approach, where the starter relates to the main body of the lesson; and the *horizontal* approach, where the starter relates to other starters. In practice, departments and teachers will mix these two methods, but it's helpful to compare them in principle.

While the notion of a string of horizontal starters – on spelling and vocabulary, for example – is organisationally tempting, it seems to me problematical. This approach creates a discrete run of mini-lessons which certainly may generate learning within themselves, but could be said to distort the shape of the lessons as a whole. It also may tend in practice towards decontextualised word- and sentence-level skills teaching, which isn't the purpose of the *Framework*. From the children's point of view, their lesson divides into parts that don't connect and value may be lost in any or all of them.

The dance between the general and the specific lies at the heart of good English teaching. Milton wrote *Paradise Lost*; he also used oxymorons. Estate agents write highly persuasive prose; they also use euphemisms. A pupil writes an exciting story about alien abduction; she also chooses the present tense. The effectiveness of our teaching lies in the ease with which we move between and resolve these focuses, and the starter which clearly offers chosen specifics to be developed and contextualised in the later lesson activities is offering a model of and a guide to those relationships. Not to use it in this way is to miss one of the major opportunities of the *Framework*.

There is another difficulty that requires some thought. Children need recaps at the beginnings of lessons. They have been through several other lessons, and other more significant experiences, since you last saw them. An initial recap establishes and re-establishes where they are with English, as well as providing an evaluation for you of your previous lesson with them. Simply saying, *Do you remember what we did last time?* isn't an exciting start, and can lead to the dreaded poor lesson beginning discussed in Chapter 5. It's also not especially reliable. Some more useful introductory recaps might be:

- discuss in pairs what happened, then feed back;
- discuss in pairs one specific teacher-asked question;
- express what happened in exactly fifteen words;
- discuss what we need to do today;
- swap your jotted one-sentence recap with someone else and combine them;
- sum up your progress in the last lesson in one sentence/word;
- sympathetic pair questioning;
- adversarial pair questioning.

(In the pair questioning, A interviews B about last lesson – sympathetically trying to draw her out, or adversarially trying to catch her out.)

The starter and the recap have to co-exist in some way. Starters which run horizontally can't easily offer whole-lesson recaps and indeed run into their own difficulties because they themselves need recaps. The vertical lesson better allows starter and recap to work together.

For example, children recall how, in the previous lesson, they saw writers using *evidence* to back up an argument. Today's starter concerns how writers use *exaggeration* for the same purpose. The starter considers exaggeration, with reference back to the previous lesson, and with reference forward to today's main tasks, which feature exaggeration and some other argumentative techniques. So the learning has a narrative throughline within a clear context, the starter doubling as recap and transition (see Chapter 5).

The *main body* of the *Framework* lesson features a series of developing activities that choreograph a movement towards confidence and independence. Reading and writing activities, for example, will typically move from teacher demonstration (to the whole class) to guided work, where the teacher works with groups, and through scaffolding activities to independence. These structures are well documented in the *Framework* and its training materials and don't need to be summarised here.

These approaches fit perfectly with the idea of a lesson story, a narrative of connected events with explicit transitions reflecting the learning objectives (see Chapters 3 and 5 in particular). The teaching which is being encouraged here is highly interactive, involving all pupils. Among other things, this is highly evaluative, since pupils are returning their understanding to the teacher almost constantly. If they aren't confident, the teacher will know immediately and will adjust on the spot. This is the true meaning of interactivity. It is much more than lively speaking and listening: it places the teacher on sustained high evaluative alert, where assessment and evaluation of learning are entirely integrated into the teaching.

It might be worth dwelling on this concept of interactivity, which is highly favoured by the *Framework*. It's tempting to think of it in terms of noisy, lively, question-and-answer teaching. You have lots of questions and games ready to deliver your objective; there will be lots of pupil contributions; so this will be a highly interactive session.

The brilliant teacher understands that true interactivity is where the teacher considers pupil responses and modifies her explanations and activities as she goes along, rather than working through her prepared questions. *To simplify, interactivity isn't just about the pupils saying a lot; it's about the teacher listening a lot.*

A powerful strain within the *Framework* is the *Reading-to-Writing* strain, which suggests progress to independent writing from the analysis of models. Almost any kind of fiction or non-fiction text may be analysed, its conventions agreed, its style and format emulated by pupils.

For example, the consideration of a frightening ghost-story text, the creation from it of a list of frightening features (use of sounds, use of darkness, use of adverbs and so on) on a flipchart at the front of the room is followed by teacher modelling and then collaborative writing on the whiteboard, with pupils contributing and drawing on the list of conventions. The sight of a teacher writing creatively at the front of the room, discussing her choices and then pupils' choices of phrases and effects is extraordinarily powerful in both defining and demystifying the creative process. It gives pupils permission to redraft and experiment; it allows them to see text as a version, not a perfect finished product; it allows them to think of text in terms of a series of author choices. These are important realisations for any secondary age group, certainly including post-16 pupils. To work with a Year 12 group on a collaborative pastiche of U. A. Fanthorpe or Emily Brontë, revising and polishing phrases and images as you go, is highly enjoyable and leads to sophisticated analysis of effects.

This reading-to-writing thread is especially important in non-fiction writing. Brilliant English teachers recognise that the literature-based curriculum is unbalanced, and non-literary work, especially non-fiction prose, can lend an air of the real world to English, which can motivate a wide range of pupils, including (for example) boys. Boys often read better than they write, and so a progression that links the two, starting from reading, within a real-world context, is likely to motivate them. Working from a prompt is useful here: Table 7.1 is based on *Framework* training materials.

You might want to consider how you would modify a sheet like this for different pupils. It would need to be discussed and modelled; in this, as in virtually everything, an example is worth a thousand explanations.

A sheet like this might be used to enable pupils to research and analyse real-world texts (including spoken texts) and begin to prepare

Table 7.1 Text-type analysis (TTA)

Text type	
Purpose • What is its purpose? • Who is it for? • How will it be used? • What kind of writing is therefore appropriate?	
Text level • Layout • Structure/organisation • Sequence	
Sentence level • Viewpoint • Prevailing tense • Active/passive voice • Typical sentence structure and length • Typical cohesion devices	
Word level • Stock words and phrases • Specialised or typical vocabulary • Elaborate/plain vocabulary choices	
Other typical features **How could this text be improved?** **Personal reactions to the text**	

their own versions. In so doing, they are understanding not only the texts they work on, but generic fundamentals about how and why texts are created – issues to consider in their own writing. There are books and resource folders full of such texts, but children are deeply suspicious of "newspaper articles" or "job advertisements" which were never real or which, if they were, haven't been real for some years. The best place for real-world materials is the real world. Information leaflets, holiday brochures, estate agents' brochures, advertising leaflets, newspapers, music download web sites, charity appeal leaflets, magazines, film trailers, radio news bulletins, information web sites, fan magazines and web sites, book-cover blurbs, game instructions – pupils are surrounded by texts, and, given the generic nature of text-type analysis, the teacher can successfully encourage them to choose ones which reflect their own interests, and which *they can analyse using a generic prompt like the one above, and subsequently emulate in creative writing of their own.* So this central *Framework* structure encourages the association of analytical and creative work, as well as the use of pupils' own enthusiasms – two allies of the brilliant teacher which we established in Chapter 2.

Text analysis of this kind can lie at the heart of much of your work, meeting many *Framework* objectives at all three levels, and serving much of the National Curriculum as well. It can become a regular base feature.

For example, Table 7.2 was completed during a medium-term plan on persuasive language with a Year 9 group. During this unit pupils analysed magazine advertisements, book and CD covers and estate agents' brochures, and (in pairs) carried out market research concerning a new product of their own devising. These products ranged from pop groups to chocolate bars and (inevitably) trainers. They created questionnaires around their new products, which were completed by class and family members concerning content, product image, appearance, name and so on. The products were then designed and publicity material was presented to the class for evaluation.

This is a simple scheme to envisage and its strength rests on the focuses and structures in the teaching. At an early stage, magazine advertisements are analysed as texts with distinct purposes, audiences and conventions. The teacher wants pupils to look through magazines and choose their own advertisements because this allows for pupil choice and opinion and because the choice of the advertisement forms the initial part of the analysis; so the prompt sheet may begin by asking the pupil why he chose his particular advertisement; it has

Table 7.2 TTA: estate agent's particulars

Text	Estate agent sales particulars
Text type	Persuasive
Purpose • What is its purpose? • Who is it for? • How will it be used? • What kind of writing is therefore appropriate?	To sell the house Prospective, interested customers They will read it at home and decide whether to take the trouble to view the house Persuasive, positive, informative, self-explanatory, reassuring, detailed, accessible
Text level • Layout • Structure/organisation • Sequence	Systematic, conventional Photograph, general description, more detailed description General description, directions, downstairs rooms, upstairs rooms, gardens
Sentence level • Viewpoint • Prevailing tense • Active/passive voice • Typical sentence structure and length • Typical cohesion devices	Third person singular, except for "directions", which are second person Present Mixture. Quite a lot of passive, eg, "the gardens are approached via a stone path" Mixture, but most sentences are long and complex, featuring many adjectival phrases and clauses. Many irregular sentences, often omitting "to be", e.g.: "Panelled door with two obscure glazed viewing panels . . ." Sentences are often lists Overall structure rather than usual cohesion features
Word Level • Stock words and phrases	"executive style" "the accommodation comprises"

Table 7.2 continued

		"spacious" "highly recommended for internal inspection" etc. etc.
• Specialised or typical vocabulary		"kitchen/breakfast room" etc. gardens at "front, side and rear" "Galleried landing" "low-level WC" "obscure double-glazed window" "front elevation" etc. euphemism e.g. "deceptively spacious"
• Elaborate/plain vocabulary choices		Mixture of factual material (a lot has to be included) and elaborate, idealised, e.g. "fronting the village green"

Other typical features

It will try to look and sound "expensive", implying the luxury of the property itself. It will use colour photography. There is a great deal of stock and specialised vocabulary. There is also small print which most people won't read.

How could this text be improved?

There needs to be more description of the garden. They need to give the sizes of the rooms, because not giving them makes us think they're probably very small. Some of the language is too flowery.

Personal reactions to the text

These are written in a poetic sort of style that puts some of us off. The euphemisms are over-the-top and actually make us less inclined to look at the houses sometimes because we are suspicious of them. We don't really trust the brochures.

already in some sense worked on him. This is much more powerful than handing out a single advert to everybody, because it's bound not to interest some of them, and this will make their analysis of its effects pointless if not impossible.

Prompt scripts prevent children from simply leafing through magazines. They will show pupils what to look for in some detail, based on earlier whole-class discussions of advertisements, target audience, product image, and so on. They will mention fonts, colour, slogans, language, sentence types, euphemisms, imagery (similes, metaphors, symbols), alliteration and so on. A good teacher will talk about these things with a class before handing out the magazines for analysis, but a brilliant teacher knows that, even after discussion of what they're looking for, pupils without a prompt script to complete will become seduced by the magazines and waste a good deal of time gazing at them. After all, that's what the magazines are meant to do. The prompt script, which is generic, allows pupil choice to be anchored to the requirements of the learning.

Similarly, written guidance on question-and-answer techniques and questionnaire structures ensure that surveying is more than a series of chats with mates. Again, these focuses are generic, so generic guidance can secure the diverse nature of the content in the room. Tight deadlines for each stage of the process also help to motivate.

At an early point, the class looked at house brochures and, working individually, then in pairs, then as a class, completed a prompt script (see Table 7.2). This is generic work: the pupil understanding that really matters is in the left-hand column. To help to secure this, pupils had already worked (in starter and main-lesson activities) on some of the left-hand concepts within a range of contexts. They had built specialist vocabulary glossaries around subjects of their own choosing, and they had swapped celebrity catch-phrases to build the idea of stock language. Then the completed sheet as above formed an exemplar for more independent analysis of further texts.

The point about using a script like this one more than once is that it introduces a uniformity that, as well as affording familiarity, focus, and security, allows significant concepts to be built within a wide variety of contexts, some of which may be pupil-chosen. This is a productive and healthy relationship between teacher prescription and pupil diversity.

Such analysis can also be applied to spoken texts. For example, the *Today's News* activity is set within a medium-term plan about purpose, audience and appropriateness of language, and begins with analysis of local radio news bulletins (see Table 7.3).

In fact, many pupils will be able to complete a good deal of this without listening to your carefully prepared tapes. They live in the world of texts like this and often know more about language than you think; but such analysis makes that knowledge explicit and therefore useable elsewhere.

Moving from the analytical to the creative phase, pupils now write at least six one-line true stories about themselves. These are NOT written in journalistic language but they must be recent and true.

Table 7.3 TTA: the news

Text type	Radio news bulletin
Purpose	
• What is its purpose?	Inform and entertain
• Who is it for?	Busy audience, local, possibly drivers
• How will it be used?	Heard, audience doing other things
• What kind of writing is therefore appropriate?	Short, attention-grabbing, variety, clarity; "live", spontaneous
Text level	
• Layout	Headlines, stories, some with interviews
• Structure/organisation	Headlines for top stories
	Stories then follow in order, each with headline or introduction, one or two with interviews
	Each story begins with a lead, attention-grabbing sentence with significant basic facts
	Each story brief, e.g. five sentences
• Sequence	Most significant stories first; sport last; stories possibly grouped e.g. local stories, national stories
Sentence level	
• Viewpoint	Newsreader; brisk recount, 3rd-person
• Prevailing tense	Varies, usually past
• Active/passive voice	Varies, usually active
• Typical sentence structure and length	Varies, usually short
• Typical cohesion devices	"Over to . . ."
	Links and introductions
	One or two voices
	Headlines
Word level	
• Stock words and phrases	Over to
	And now for something different
	Jane, 32, a factory worker from Worcester
	Friends said that
	Top story today

Table 7.3 continued

	Finally Now for some light relief A major incident A spokesman said

• Specialised or typical
  vocabulary
• Elaborate/plain
  vocabulary choices
	(Above)
	Spokesman
	Plain, but dramatic. Alliteration, puns

Other typical features

Brief, attention-grabbing descriptions; highly formulaic

How could this text be improved?

The delivery is very shouty and very little detail is given. The stories are so local they often aren't interesting if you don't actually know the people. They could be slightly longer, and choose slightly fewer stories, and give more detail.

Personal reactions to the text

Quite a few of us do listen to local radio but we tend to ignore the news; some of the stories are pointless. We don't like the funny "and finally" stories because usually they aren't funny. However, local news is sometimes necessary.

They write such things as *Ahmed missed the first bus to school this morning* or *Julie did the washing-up again on Sunday*. The stories are written on strips of paper, at least six per pupil.

The strips are torn up into individual one-line stories and thrown into a box. Pupils form into groups. Each group is a radio station local to the school or the class. News strips are thrown randomly at the groups and they have to turn them into a three-minute news bulletin. To do this they must:

• choose six stories;
• write the stories for broadcasting, using the conventions from the analysis script;
• place the stories in order, using the analysis script;
• rehearse the presentation, including jingles, cohesion devices, and so on;
• perform their bulletins.

This is a hectic and enjoyable activity that should be begun and ended in one hour – the sense of deadline adds a realistic, news-room pressure that is highly motivating. It is light-hearted in its content – the stories are comical precisely because they are essentially true, and children enjoy the counterpoint between mundane content and dramatic presentation. This counterpoint, as well as being funny, draws attention to the generic features of news broadcasting language precisely because of its incongruity. They easily slip into: *Julie, 14, a student and part-time rabbit-fancier from Abingdon, was devastated by the filthy state of the frying pan, but commented bravely, "It was hard scrubbing, but somebody had to do it!" Friends say that Julie is now resting and recovering.* In so doing, they are learning serious lessons about texts, conventions, genre, journalism and values.

So this central reading-to-writing thread is highly beneficial in many ways, but it must be used to explore and extend, rather than to confirm that writers know how to do it and we don't; and the only way for us to learn is by copying them. The most productive analysis is critical, not merely passive. For example, understanding how advertisements work includes understanding how they seek to deceive. And part of our analysis needs to be about improving the original in some way, not seeing it as a platonic ideal to be imitated. When pupils suggest relevant additions to an RSPCA leaflet, they are showing embedded and personal understanding. So the final two fields in the analysis scripts quoted above are very important in extending and consolidating learning and, of course, in introducing pupil opinion to liven up the analysis.

This element of the personal is perhaps an issue with the *Framework*. One of its training videos shows young pupils discussing a leaflet about cruelty to animals; this is a guided reading activity, with the teacher working with a group to analyse the purpose and techniques of the text. The leaflet is meant to shock: as one little girl says, quite correctly and entirely without emotion, "It uses emotive language."

There is something almost chilling about watching young children discussing animal cruelty and, indeed, emotions connected with it, while showing no emotion whatsoever themselves. The analytical inclinations of the *Framework* have to be balanced by materials and activities which re-introduce the pupils to the content of the work. As I have said, pupil opinion is extremely motivating. In the end, pupils have to feel things about texts at a personal level if they are fully to understand the craft of the writing and brilliant teachers will always plan opportunities for pupil choice, reaction and opinion into their *Framework* lessons.

The *plenary* is extremely valuable, providing opportunities for interactive consolidation and teacher-evaluation of learning objectives. It is discussed in detail throughout Chapter 6. The best plenaries I've seen are those that form staging posts between lessons, looking both backwards and forwards, evaluating the learning that's just taken place and therefore making suggestions about the learning that's coming next.

Some notes on literacy

People learn aspects of literacy best when the learning includes discussions of motives and effects. A starter may offer a list of sentences and invite children to divide it into two lists, distinguishing between active and passive verbs. They will learn, or appear to learn, how to recognise them. But a few minutes' discussion of why "the charity box was stolen from the chip-shop counter" (A) is different in its feel from "someone stole the charity box from the chip-shop counter" (B), and which is better, and why you might choose either, is going to anchor the point much more firmly. There will be a range of opinions:

- A puts the charity box in charge of the sentence, and that's the most important thing; or,
- B starts weakly; or,
- you don't know who stole it, so A makes better sense; or,
- B is better because you're looking for that Someone,

and so on. There are no right answers here, just an understanding that grammar affects readers. These distinctions can be quite subtle and challenging. I asked a Year 10 group why estate agents say "the house is set back from the road" instead of "the builder set the house back from the road" and received some fascinating answers. Obviously we want the house to be driving the sentence; we don't know or care who the builder was, so there's little point in mentioning him. One pupil said that the more passive construction, removing the builder from the picture, established the house almost as a part of nature, just there, like the trees, and this creates a sense of peace and rightness which is highly persuasive.

Positive models

Thirty years ago I could spell. I could spell *surprise* without having to think about it. Now, I have to pause briefly every time I write it and remember whether there's an *r* before the *p*.

This may of course be the onset of dementia, brought about by a longish career in teaching; but it's mainly because I've seen *suprise* so many times that it's become imprinted. We mustn't underestimate the importance of the visual. We don't sound out a word like *right-eousness*; we know it by seeing it; so we must be careful that pupils see plenty of good models when we're building literacy.

For example, the best way I've found of teaching specific points of punctuation has been emphatically *not* the presentation of blocks of text with the punctuation "removed" for the pupils to "fill in". I still see this ancient practice on a regular basis. I did it at school myself. It makes me nervous, because I don't want pupils staring at incorrect models; in the end, it may be the models, not their corrections, that they remember.

The use of a research model around good texts is not only theoretically more positive; it's also the most effective classroom method I've found in practice. You decide that the class needs work on speech marks – because it's in the plan, or because you've noted in your marking that this is an issue. Present the pupils with a well-chosen paragraph of conversation – perhaps from the class reader. Explain that they need a better understanding of how a professional author uses speech marks. In pairs, they will discuss the passage and sketch out the rules for speech marks as exemplified here, knowing that what they're looking at is good practice. I usually provide a list of prompting questions – where do speech marks actually go? (Comic-strip speech bubbles is a good analogy). How do the speech marks affect the reader? What other punctuation goes with them? Where does that go? When are capital letters used?

This last question causes enduring difficulty and the best answer is: capital letters go at the beginnings of sentences (as we know) and, in speech, the writer obviously has his own sentences but the *speakers have their own sentences as well*. This explains

Henry said, "There's no time for this."

And also

"There's nothing here," said Misha, "that we need to take away."

Having worked in pairs to answer the rules-questions, the class convenes to build a joint guide to using speech marks – posters, leaflets or a web site for other classes, with heavy guidance from the teacher. The work proceeds by investigation and deduction.

The irritating survival of the apostrophe

The apostrophe is slowly dying, and the end can't come soon enough for me. Like a decaying auntie, it's possessive, demanding, difficult, and rarely tells you anything you don't already know. Nevertheless, for the time being we're stuck with it – the single most confusing punctuation mark and, I have to say, the most badly taught.

Literate, hard-working sixth-formers (and indeed postgraduates) still worry about the possessive apostrophe; they still quite often write *mens'* or *childrens'*, and tell you solemnly that it's because it's a

plural. The single most effective thing to tell children about posses-
sion is that *the rule is always the same*. Plurality makes absolutely no
difference (but it's nearly always cited and nearly always causes
confusion). *The apostrophe is placed after the noun* – after the owner;
this is always right, and almost all you need to know (but not quite).

So the owner of the toilets is the men, so we write *men's toilets*.
The owner of the playground is the children, so *children's playground*. The owner of the phone is Rosie, so *Rosie's phone*. Teach
children this one rule and leave it with them. Don't bring in a lot
of stuff about plurals. At a later stage, when you know that this is
embedded, you can extend it by pointing out that words that already
end in *s* usually don't bother with a second one as in *the Smiths'
holiday*, *Keats' poetry*.

It's a cliché (because it's true) that when you're trying to clear up
a confusion, you shouldn't deal with all of the constituent parts of it
– it will only cement the confusion; and yet we do it all the time.
Trying to separate *their* and *there* by carefully going over the
differences with the class may feel right, but within a week the
confusions will return, rejuvenated by your help. Choose one and
deal with it – <u>there</u> is the opposite of <u>here</u>, etc. Leave the other alone.
Don't even mention it. It is a completely different thing – that's the
point. There are lots of reasons for putting *s* on the end of an English
word (presumably because *s* is easy to say on the end of any word.
Try adding *t* or *p* to the end of a word and pronouncing it). Going
through all of these at once (possessives, plurals, third-person
singulars) in an attempt to clear it all up will just add to the mess. Deal
with one issue. Examine it, contextualise it, evaluate the learning
over a period (for example, by focused setting and marking of written
work, not by tests).

The *Framework* supports the range and variety of learning styles,
the genuine interactivity, the explicit basis in objectives, the central
and active role of the teacher and other adults, which all contribute
to excellent practice. Like all educational initiatives it undergoes
constant review and humanisation by the teachers who implement it,
and needs to be treated with respect rather than reverence, but it's a
significant asset in your quest to be a brilliant teacher.

Chapter 8

Working with big texts

The moment when Scout Finch realises that her night-time rescuer is none other than Boo Radley, the man she taunted for years, is an annual delight for me. However many times I read it aloud to Year 10, Scout's "Hey, Boo", brings a catch to my throat, as so many of the book's pressures are gently and astonishingly released, and the pupils realise, one by one, what's happened. Shared moments like that remain central to the life of a classroom. Listening together to a novel may be as close as some of your pupils get to the enhancing experience of being in a theatre audience, of being an individual and part of a community at the same time. That on its own is sufficient to underwrite the survival of the class reader.

There are other, more overtly differentiated ways of working with large texts to meet individual needs and interests, but I see no sign of the disappearance of the shared text. The right class novel is a major asset; it improves learning, relationships and behaviour. Year 7 or Year 8 want nothing more than to come to English to read *Skellig*; poorly motivated Year 10 groups start to ask if they can carry on with *Of Mice and Men*. The choice of a good novel or play can be profoundly healing.

Perhaps because of this, the class reader has dominated the English curriculum. A few years ago, if you asked an English teacher what he was doing with Year 8, he would reply, "*Tom's Midnight Garden*, then *A Midsummer Night's Dream*". Certainly the *Framework* has confirmed a movement towards more balance, helping the brilliant English teacher to think and plan carefully and selectively around large texts, recognising some of the dilemmas that surround them.

Of course, there's the major issue of the integration of texts into the rest of the English curriculum. For years this was a matter of "spin-offs", and teachers became ingenious at delivering all sorts of English content with reference to the class reader. It was not uncommon for a pupil's entire English experience for weeks at a time to be derived from a novel or play – which was fine, if he happened to like it, and it happened to offer appropriate learning. It's perfectly legitimate to use a text as a resource: it offers rich contexts; but what matters is that this work is wide-ranging, driven by developmental objectives rather than literary opportunism, and complemented by other work.

The text is an enormous and energetic resource with its own momentum. On the one hand, it offers many gifts to the teacher that are individual to itself. The relationship of George and Lennie is something with which GCSE-age pupils have an instinctive affinity. It is both accessible and rich – a rare combination, the Holy Grail of textual study. Tom Robinson's trial is riveting, Offred's deliberate narrative is hypnotic; the structure of *An Inspector Calls* is both bizarre and concrete; these are areas to enjoy and to study. The worst thing to do with any text is to twist it into a set of generic learning objectives that pay little attention to its individual qualities, its particular gifts to you as a teacher. And yet the traditional model of text plus spin-offs isn't good enough when we are trying to construct developmental and progressive learning.

There's one further conundrum. Although the National Curriculum barely mentions it, pleasure is a literary principle; we want our pupils to enjoy books. This is the main motivator in literary reading and must be central to choosing texts and designing work around them. There's nothing frivolous about this: it's extremely difficult to make useful critical judgments about a book that you find pointless. You can't decide whether the ending of *Wuthering Heights* is satisfactory if, frankly, you find the entire book unsatisfying. If literary appreciation begins with personal response (see Chapter 4), then it helps if that response is appreciative in some degree. At the same time, however, teachers have to prepare pupils for examinations in set books, and this is not a process guaranteed to provoke happiness.

Answering these questions isn't particularly difficult. It requires the teacher to be aware of them, to address them in her planning, and to resist the temptations to (on the one hand) reduce the novel or play to character study and exams or (on the other hand) allow it to determine the entire English agenda for the next twelve weeks.

Medium-term planning ensures that the right text is chosen with regard to pupil involvement, the gifts of the text, and its integration via learning objectives with the rest of the work. For example, a

GCSE text is chosen against assessment objectives (AOs) within the exam specification. The teacher should not proceed to write her medium-term plan without firstly considering those criteria in book-specific terms. You might write some preliminary notes connecting Steinbeck's *Of Mice and Men* with the objectives for GCSE English Literature such as these:

AO1 respond to texts critically, sensitively and in detail, selecting appropriate ways to convey their response, using textual evidence as appropriate

Essay work, use of quotations to support opinions, essay structure; appropriate vocabulary

AO2 explore how language, structure and forms contribute to the meanings of texts, considering different approaches to texts and alternative interpretations

The dream theme; the George/Lennie relationship; the minorities theme (The wife, Crooks). The descriptive passages opening chapters 1 and 2; the parallels (mice/men; dog/Lennie); the films, especially the film openings and portrayal of Curly's wife (is she a slut? etc); the ending (alternative endings, is it satisfactory? A shock?); character language and idiolect; contrasts e.g. Slim and Curly

AO3 explore relationships and comparisons between texts, selecting and evaluating relevant material

Compare use of third-person narrative with To Kill a Mockingbird *(first person); watch and compare with film* Rain Man *(relationships)*

AO4 relate texts to their social, cultural and historical contexts and literary traditions.

Research project on Great Depression; look at Grapes of Wrath *and contemporary newspaper sources; language of book*

This is straightforward, and often it's where initial planning stops; but it's only the first of three sets of criteria. You have determined how the book specifically addresses the assessment objectives. But you need also to consider:

- What are the gifts of the book in terms of pupil enjoyment and learning?
- How does the book connect with the rest of the work?

Brilliant teachers place a high premium on the enjoyment of a shared text. A novel or play is a big thing – it will be with you for weeks and it can change the entire atmosphere of your classroom. Having outlined briefly the kind of study that will serve the assessment objectives, you need to pause and consider where the pleasure is (and this is your estimation of the pupils' pleasure, not your own). You might for example decide that your pupils will definitely enjoy studying the relationship of George and Lennie (they always do); the dream theme (because they can identify with this, all adolescents have dreams of a better future); the film comparisons (because they will be able to offer opinions); discussion of the ending (because it's brutal and usually unexpected); discussion of Curly's wife (opinions in an intriguingly sexy area). However, you might also conclude that there are some low-pleasure zones here. The research on the Great Depression doesn't look very exciting; they don't know what an idiolect is; reading extracts, while worthy and relevant, is probably a dull thing to be doing.

You need also to check that your notes cover the significant gifts of the book. For example, I haven't mentioned above the story, the slow build-up of tension, the ominousness of Curly and (differently) his wife, the prevailing sense right from the beginning that these men will not achieve their dream: these are all powerfully involving features of the book, offering strong teaching potential, but it's possible to miss them if you're only governed by generic assessment objectives. So it's vital that your preliminary planning goes beyond simply meeting the assessment criteria and back to the book, devising activities which maximise the pleasurable learning opportunities offered by the text.

Idiolect

You also need to consider how the text relates to the rest of the work. For example, the characters may have their own ways of talking. Scout and Jem have their own ways of swearing, and there are words like *bindle* in *Of Mice and Men* that pupils won't know. You might want them to study how this vocabulary adds to the authenticity of the books' worlds by linking to a complete set of language study centred on the idea of *idiolect*.

Of itself, the idiolect work scheme is immensely useful. It involves pupils drawing conclusions about their own language and requires them to investigate and understand a wide range of significant language issues. They will consider the notions of dialect, of language change, of language influences, of grammar and vocabulary variations, of personal language habits, of coherence.

The power of the idiolect work is that it considers these potentially quite abstract, linguistic concepts via discussion of the pupil's own language. The abstract is made personal; adolescents like talking about themselves; the investigation of language becomes a kind of self-discovery. Over a period of weeks they carry out research that enables them to make two statements:

- I speak like this; *and*
- This is why I speak like this.

The work is summed up in Table 8.1.

Through a process of research based on surveying friends, teachers and family, the pupil reaches some conclusions about her speech habits. She tries to account for them by considering how she is influenced; and she produces a final outcome which may be a written project or a presentation.

This is valuable work in itself; but it works very well alongside the study of language in a novel or play. The book, or characters within it, may have their own idiolects. Considering why Mr Bounderby or Offred or Snowball talk the way they do is enriched and informed by this separate study of related concepts. This goes beyond spin-off into planning, where major components of the work link productively against learning objectives, that are clear in the teacher's mind and that, though usually based on assessment objectives, go beyond them if necessary.

How to kill a novel

The principle of enjoying the book should remain at the centre of your thinking as you plan and carry out the teaching. This has straightforward, practical implications. Don't watch a film first: the story is the major impetus; don't give away the ending. Don't always link the book to work. Don't read it for too long – twenty minutes

Table 8.1 Idiolect

My personal language

Influences	Language habits
My nationality	Quiet or loud?
My family	Reserved or talkative?
My geographical area	Home-made words?
My friends	Favourite words?
My teachers	Lots of questions?
My role models	Hesitations?
My personal interests	Repetitions? *etc.*
My personality	

Research	Project
Discussion with friends	Prose account of personal language:
Discussion with family	Descriptions in prose,
Discussion with teachers	transcripts, charts,
Tape-recordings	connecting language to
Pair work	influences.
Drama work	
Role plays	Oral or written presentation
School books	

is long enough, and at the end of the lesson is better than at the beginning – pupils relaxing, the book not a chore to be got through, the preliminary to more work, but a well-earned reward. Don't ever read around the class. Don't you remember that? *Jane Eyre* being serially murdered, the voice of the book changing unaccountably, people and meaning getting lost together in that slow meander around the room. You may well need to hear pupils reading the text, to evaluate their understanding, but you can use better structures –

pupils reading characters, or pupils alternating with you. Don't do chapter summaries – there is always something better than this. Prepare your reading and try to use your voice a little to show character and mood. Edit the text if necessary, and don't start at the beginning if it's not the best place. (I gave up reading *To Kill a Mockingbird* several times because of the opening few pages). Don't rely on the pupils doing massive amounts of personal reading, and, if you do set reading for homework, you need to be able to check that it's been done – most certainly not by setting a test. (For example, set a homework which involves reading a passage and preparing a specific discussion topic from it.)

How to kill a play

A play isn't a novel with an odd layout. Of course, you can study the hierarchy of plot, character, relationship, theme, style and structure, as with novels, but to recognise that plays are fundamentally different is to open up a range of exciting extra teaching opportunities; and to fail to recognise it is to create pitfall after pitfall. And yet this happens so often. I've marked countless GCSE and A-level answers on dramatic texts that talk about "the reader" and describe stage directions as "narration".

Reading a play is an unnatural act. It makes little more sense than reading a symphonic score, and requires a similar act of imagination.

The words were written to be heard and seen, not read. The reader (teacher or student) has to imagine herself to be a member of the audience; only then can she begin to appreciate the function and structure of what she's reading.

When the pupil sees the play from this perspective (being frequently helped and reminded to do so) she can begin to ask new questions, and to answer old questions in new ways. What does a play do that a novel doesn't? The answers have far-ranging implications for good teaching.

While both probably last several weeks in the classroom, a play in the real world lasts for about two hours. A pupil at the half-way point of *An Inspector Calls* needs to be thinking in terms not of five weeks' study but of one hour's watching if she is to appreciate what the text is doing. This basic compression lies at the heart of understanding the play's structure. The audience experiences the play aurally, visually and linearly; they cannot pause, they cannot decide to read for twenty minutes and make a cup of tea; they cannot re-read a forgotten section. They are a captive audience. So structural issues like juxtaposition become crucial in understanding plays. As scene three begins, the closing words of scene two are literally still ringing in our ears; the playwright can force contrast or confirmation as he controls our experience. In this sense, he has more direct power over us than a novelist does.

He can force dramatic irony on us, and this is a brilliant area for teaching. Dramatic irony is a sophisticated structural weapon for a playwright, but it's extremely easy to understand, and so is a key area for moving pupils to higher learning. It is present in soap operas, comedies, horror films: popular culture would be lost without it. A man in a white coat comes in; the housewife begins to undress. It's funny (possibly, if you like this sort of thing) because we know he's a plumber, we know she thinks he's a doctor, we know that he doesn't know that. Dramatic irony is simply about layers of knowledge, and can always be hierarchically mapped, as thus:

- audience
- plumber
- woman

The audience isn't always at the top: when Edmund tells us that he has a plot against his father, Gloucester, he doesn't tell us what the plot is; so the dramatic irony map is:

- Edmund
- audience
- Gloucester

But the audience is always part of the map, and understanding their reaction is understanding what the writer is doing.

Some plays begin with elaborate set descriptions. These are not "narration" but clear instructions to the director and designer. The pupil can only understand them when she considers them as instructions to create initial and then sustained effects on the audience. This set is what the playwright wants the audience to see as it settles into its seats and makes its preliminary judgments about what it's in for over the next two hours. Of course, sketching it is a good activity, but (as always) it's a better activity when it's focused and when the objective is clear. As the lights go up at the opening of *Death of a Salesman*, what do you see? What judgments do you make (as all audiences always do) about what the play is going to be like?

The playwright doesn't have "narration", he can't offer prose commentaries on his characters' thoughts and motives, so understanding moments like the first appearances of characters makes sense when we think of how the audience is being influenced. When we first see the colonial officers in *Our Country's Good*, they are shooting birds – apparently their immediate response to the fauna of the beautiful new land they've come to colonise. The playwright has to make points quickly and visually. As always, comparison is the teacher's friend here; the officers could have been playing chess, or dining, and discussion of the writer's choice (how would it have been different?) leads quickly to the notion of symbolism. Symbolism may be a high-level, esoteric study in poetry or novels, but in plays it's virtually constant. The audience is looking and judging all the time. Working with text transformation is a useful way of understanding these differences. To rewrite a piece of prose as drama is to see what tools the playwright needs to use to generate audience reaction. What symbolic structures might be used instead of prosaic author commentary? Try working with a scene of (for example) Shakespeare and introducing different background activities. The characters are talking of love, but they're also playing squash, or watching TV, or doing the ironing. The teacher works constantly to expand the pupil's imagination in terms of seeing the text.

How is this work achieved? The sense that we must imagine ourselves into the theatre in order to experience a play and so be able to appreciate it can be at almost every level of teaching. At its most formal and structural, it involves actually going to the theatre, which is immensely valuable but far from sufficient. As ever, clear objectives and related follow-up are vital. Give pupils focuses for their visit (without ruining their evenings with worksheets) and discuss these afterwards. These will be interpretative focuses – how do they play the aborigine? Is the set as you imagined it? Is Willy played as a fool or a hero? Do you like the modern dress? The subsequent discussion is vital – you have no control over the production, you don't know if it will be enhancing of itself; if it isn't, it becomes your job in follow-up to make it valuable. Weeks of study which fails to consistently address the dramatic nature of the text cannot be salvaged by hiring a bus and taking most of the pupils to the theatre. The visit has meaning only when set within a lively context of theatrical responses.

So classroom study must be habitually dramatic, to support the theatre visit if it finally comes, to substitute for it if it doesn't. Practical drama work can explore interpretations of various scenes, themes and techniques. Classroom teaching at every level can pay attention to audience and effects. A formal scheme of work on *Director's Notes* emphasises the centrality of interpretation, the idea that a play isn't the reading out of dialogue, the significance of creative opinion.

The *Notes* are simply the notes that a director might make in framing a production. They can take the form of written and sketched instructions to set designers, musicians, lighting staff, actors and costume designers, setting out (perhaps) a consistent view of the play. Pupils can work in pairs, and they can prepare presentations and rationales for their visions.

These are quite large pieces of teaching, but they need underpinning by routines. Pupils should run the play on their imaginary stages as their normal response to classroom reading. I've seen teachers actually present seating plans to classes and encourage pupils to choose a seat, decide whom they're next to, and remember the seat number in future lessons. Frequent classroom pauses allow pupils to consider what they're seeing at any given moment. Keeping a play log enables them to sketch regularly how characters are, in their imaginations, placed on the stage; how the stage is lit at the moment; if they're reminded of any earlier scenes; what questions the current scene is raising in their minds; who is looking at whom; who is standing closest to the audience, and so on.

Texts and examinations

Don't do repeated examination preparation. I have marked thousands of GCSE and A-level literature scripts and it's absolutely clear to me that pupils who show confident enjoyment of texts do better than those with prepared and formulaic answers. Of course you will need to practise in the final stages of an examination course, but the study of the text is much more than that. In the end, you can't predict examination questions, but you can structure your work to ensure that pupils will be flexible and versatile when the awful day comes. So let's consider the stages of teaching a class reader which lead a GCSE pupil towards that buoyant examination performance without sacrificing even more important values.

You might want to prepare pupils to write an examination or coursework essay about the theme of hopes and dreams in *Of Mice and Men*, and so understanding this theme (and, perhaps, the nature of themes in general) is your initial learning objective.

Thematic understanding is central to examination work at GCSE level. It's helpful to think in terms of a hierarchy of topics at this level; roughly speaking, this hierarchy is:

Structure
Style
Theme

Relationship
Character
Plot

It's approximately true to say that movement up this hierarchy represents movement to more sophisticated understanding of texts; and also to higher marks in examinations. Basic GCSE answers might deal with plot, for example in terms of important incidents from the story. Character work is certainly available to most GCSE pupils, and this quite easily merges into discussion of relationships. But there is a clear horizontal line within this hierarchy, between Relationship and Theme, and it's the line beyond which we stop talking about the book as if it were a true account of real life and start understanding it as a construction, a piece of art, a series of writer choices. The moment we stop explaining Heathcliff or Curly in terms of their upbringing or personality and begin to see that Heathcliff is as he is partly because he contrasts with Linton, and Curly is necessary to the plot, and so on, is a key moment in pupils' responses to texts. It's also the moment when their grades enter the A and B range.

One of the major advantages of a text like *Of Mice and Men* is that it provides access for a wide range of pupils to the higher parts of this hierarchy. Pupils who aren't obviously literary can quite easily see key points of structure; they can see that the shooting of the dog is related to the shooting of Lennie. The brilliant teacher chooses and teaches texts in a way which allow most or all of her pupils, not just the very clever ones, to access the higher understanding. One of the ways to travel there is by remembering the significance of pupil journeys *from the personal to the formal* and *from the concrete to the abstract*.

Theme stands as a staging point in the middle of the hierarchy and is a place where pupils can go beyond basic plot and character to looking at the book as a constructed whole while still dealing comfortably with content rather than technique. It's a half-way point, and a good starting point for many pupils.

So, to return to our example, you want to study the theme of hopes and dreams in *Of Mice and Men*.

Of course, you can "do" the text (see Chapter 4). You can stop at key points and discuss them while pupils make notes and then write about them. You have already planned the key issues, after all. But a brilliant teacher crafts lessons that provide experiences for pupils, not just notes, and that lead pupils to personal recognition as well as understanding. As ever, what matters is the planning focus.

In this example, you need to clarify what you mean by *dream*. There's a temptation here to veer into historical research about the "American Dream" and I've read many a GCSE answer that wasted pages on this. Background is fine, but it belongs in the background. The point about the dream is precisely not that it was a phenomenon of a particular place (not here) and a particular time (not now) but that it has to do with us now, as readers. Although I'm using an example here (from the most popular of all GCSE texts), this principle is universal. Themes are by definition transferable, and this means they may be transferred to the pupils' experience.

This principle guides you straight into a simple structure such as that shown in Table 8.2. The lesson begins with pair discussion, then whole-class discussion, all centred on the notion that what you dream about indicates what's missing from your life. The movement from concrete to abstract is easy – if you want a games console, you lack a games console; but if you want a holiday, you lack something else – freedom, rest, pleasure, excitement. Equally easy is the move-ment from personal understanding to understanding the text. In fact, the *rabbits* dream is quite complex and, in reading it carefully in order to complete the table, we discover a wide range of abstracts that are issues in the book as a whole. George and Lennie lack com-fort, autonomy, independence, warmth, relationship, responsibility, stability . . .

This table is a simple focusing structure that links the text to the pupils' personal understanding so that they can write about it with

Table 8.2 *Of Mice and Men*: dreams

I dream of	I lack
a hi-fi	a hi-fi
a pet	warmth companionship
a holiday	rest adventure excitement
George and Lennie dream of	**They lack**
rabbits	warmth companionship responsibility hope
a stove	warmth stability self-sufficiency decent food
a house	pride status stability autonomy comfort
land	food comfort status inependence freedom
vegetables	
staying at home when it rains	

some authority. Like most textual study, it centres on speaking and listening, using discussion to set out, revise and improve concepts. It is work that is done as you read the text, probably at the first or second iteration of the *rabbits* dream, and produces structured notes that record conversation and understanding and await processing into a piece of examination writing. Of course, the final written assignment won't include the pupil's hi-fi aspirations; the movement towards formality is another of the movements that the teacher has to manage. The work was chosen to reflect one of the gifts of the book – the theme of the dream, which is not only central to the text but a theme that adolescents are likely to respond to.

So, as you work through a class text, you are pausing for structured lessons that focus on central issues that you've chosen in your planning not only to service assessment objectives but to carry the text towards the pupils (or vice-versa). This requires planning decisions and the courage to select. There's no doubt that focus in textual study helps pupils write confidently about a text, even if, in the event, they aren't writing about one of the focus areas. Focus areas help pupils to hold the text – *1984* or *To Kill a Mockingbird* is a long read; each may occupy months in the classroom; pupils need throughlines to connect the end of the book (in March) with the beginning (last January). The gifts of *Of Mice and Men* are: the relationship; the tension; the sense of fate; the accessible structure, the dream. *Animal Farm* has people as animals; the seven-commandments structure; revolution in the real world. *To Kill a Mockingbird* has Scout's narration; the growing-up theme; the trial; the social themes; the connection of the two plots (they're both about prejudice).

Text activities

Don't forget DARTs (Chapter 4) when teaching a full-length text. For example, you can pause a class text for a brief deletions exercise that draws attention to the author's use of metaphor. DARTs aren't confined to the study of small texts and poetry.

In fact there is a wide range of activities based on creative understanding of the text. For example, you are likely to want to consider the opening of a text, and to talk about what book beginnings need to do. This is a direct, approachable, discursive piece of purpose-and-audience analysis, and teachers do it often. *Do the opening paragraphs provide enough of the right kind of information to make you want to read on?* This is strong work, because it evokes pupil opinion; but if applied only to one book – the book which, frankly, we all know we're going to read anyway, whatever we say about its opening – it's not really a living opinion. As ever, comparison is your main ally. Making a short work-scheme out of looking at the beginnings of *several* books and choosing one against agreed book-beginning criteria is a more genuine kind of activity. It's especially powerful if in some sense the choice being made is real. Certainly with Year 8 and Year 9 classes I have allowed these to be genuine choices of whole-class readers. Year 10 and Year 11 can choose per-sonal reading from such an activity. When pupils realise that they are actually choosing a book to work on for the next few weeks, they take their analytical and discursive responsibilities very seriously!

Other comparisons are available to help you with your analysis of the book's opening. For example, there are a number of films of *Of Mice and Men*, and none begins where the novel begins. Remember that *the sequencing of such work to provoke progressive and uncon-taminated analysis is paramount*. Here we have various pieces of material – the book opening, the openings of two or three films; and of course the pupil's own creative opinion. A brilliant teacher, rather than just reading the opening, looking at the film clips and discussing them, thinks carefully about the order of events, and about the pupils' opinions as valid material that must be part of the plan.

For example, if you show a flim clip, it will hijack the pupils' imagination. It happens to us all. I can't think of Atticus Finch as anyone other than the magnificent Gregory Peck, which is fine if I'm not trying to form my own opinions about him. There are other ways to play him – as less conciliatory, perhaps, or more brusque – but even now, if you've seen the film, you're struggling to see past it. You have the precious few moments before they see the film to establish some personal visions; so you should consider (for example) reading the opening and then story-boarding your own beginning. Pupils will almost never think at this point of starting "their" films at a completely different point – for example, with George and Lennie being chased out of Weed. So their own work provides a basis for comparison with the film clips that they will now see have taken a much more radical approach than they did. Without the stage of their own story-boarding, they will simply watch and accept with no living sense of the director's creative decisions.

Of course, you are working from learning objectives. By con-sidering the film versions of the book's opening, you are making judgments about the book. You are considering why Steinbeck starts where he does. In a sense, he doesn't start at the beginning: he recalls the Weed episode, never in much detail; and what matters here is pupil opinion. Why do the films move the opening? Which is better? Where did you put it? How do Steinbeck's creative decisions affect you as reader? Would you prefer the book a different way? Having pupils write *Chapter Minus One* – the chapter before Chapter One, where they try to deduce what happened before the beginning, and perhaps also emulate the style of the original – helps the discussion. We don't wholly know what happened. Why doesn't he tell us? Answering such questions is fundamental analysis of a writer's method, but here as so often it arises from a mixture of opinion and creativity.

The idea of story-boarding sections of your own film-of-the-book is useful in considering mood, theme, viewpoint, reaction. Analysing a few existing video clips will help pupils to see that (for example) the camera doesn't rest on the speaker, but cuts away to reaction shots. This is highly productive when considering the reactions of characters. For example, reaction shots during a long Shakespearian speech bring alive the idea of a world where people are affected by (for example) what King Lear or King Henry has to say, even if they don't (and perhaps daren't) speak. Keeping a play alive in the minds of a class is a visual business as much as an aural one. What are people feeling as Lear divides the kingdom? (Excitement, greed, fear, astonishment, pity . . . ?)

Prediction is absolutely central to enjoying and understanding a large text. Prediction is what we do with narrative; as we read, we run a commentary of predictions about who killed whom, what someone is about to do, why, what they might have meant, who's about to walk in, will they find out and how . . . Working with questions of the film-trailer variety (and in fact designing film trailers) is helpful in establishing this dynamic. It's interesting to take a section of narrative and consider what questions it asks and what questions it answers; pupils can make two columns. The proportion varies, and it's tempting to say that more questions are asked at the beginning than the end. Beginning questions are:

- Who are these men?
- Where have they come from?
- Why are they together?
- Where are they going?
- What are they carrying?

- Why are they sleeping in the open air?
- Where are they?
- When are they?

and so on. But endings can be addressed by questions too:

- Why did he do that?
- What other choices did he have?
- Should he have done that?
- Will he go to jail now?
- What will Curly do next?
- Will George give himself up?

Discussing the different kinds of questions that a text asks and answers takes you to an understanding of narrative structure and coherence and particularly of the ways in which a writer engages a reader through anticipation. This can apply to any text. A good teacher asks these questions, but a brilliant teacher has the pupils devising them as well as answering them.

Pupil prediction is always relevant and involving. It provides a basis for comparison – if things turn out differently, you can consider why the writer made different choices to you. Predicting in *Of Mice and Men* can include discussing at an early stage whether the rabbits dream will ever come true. Some hope that it will, but most pupils sense that it won't. This leads directly from pupil opinion to analysis of the text – what is it about the story that makes us take this fatalistic view? It can also involve predicting the ending from about half-way through. In fact a running prediction, right from the first chapter, is fascinating in reaching an understanding of how a text manipulates its readers. Pupils will change their views of how the book will end. The pupil who says at the outset, "Yes, I think they'll get the house and the rabbits" but is less sure half-way through needs to consider what it is about the development of the narrative, the events and prevailing atmosphere, even the structure, that has changed her mind. The whole class can run a shared prediction that they modify weekly, with reasons, in a class discussion. The teacher writes it on the wall and changes it each week after discussion. Remember, predictions provide both a basis for comparison and an engaging hook for the reader who wants to see if he was right.

There are many such activities that can be lifted off the peg and used on a text, but what matters always is not the activity but the reason for its choice, and (therefore) what you intend to do with the results. Of course, you can choose a DART and this will provoke some useful discussion, but, in order to integrate it into a developing programme of understanding, you have to be clear why you chose it. Why is deletions a better activity than sequencing or annotation or column analysis for this extract? Where is it leading? The random and occasional picking of activities provides variety and is a common model; perhaps this is why teachers will often draw a sharp line between this and the "real" work of preparing for exams. DARTs and recreative activities are an essential part of that preparation, not a holiday from it.

For example, you may put characters on trial, an activity that can range from virtually spontaneous hot-seating (Macbeth meets the press) to elaborately prepared full-scale trials with the full panoply of prepared prosecution, defence and witness statements. George can be tried for shooting Lennie; you can run Tom Robinson's appeal hearing (posthumously, I suppose); but you can also try characters not involved in crime. You can accuse Jane Eyre of being a wimp, Cordelia of being a trouble-maker, Ralph Clark of being a hypocritical social climber, Willy Loman of never growing up. Such activities will have pupils mining the texts for evidence and implication but are only fully justified when linked to progressive learning and clear outcomes. They may be linked to character work (the keeping of character fact-files as you read is very helpful), they may be linked to the style of the text or to the idea that texts may be interpreted in different ways. You may particularly want pupils to consider the true nature of blame as it relates to the world of the book. You may want pupils to appreciate that a text works on different levels (so he's both guilty and innocent) and so on.

What happens next marks out the brilliant teacher. You try Willy Loman for being a coward who confuses material well-being with happiness, a self-deluded dupe of the American Dream, a bad father and husband. The character research during the preparation will be exhaustive. The day comes, and pupils play their parts of defence, prosecution, Willy and other characters as witnesses, all of which have been prepared through the week. You are the judge (if you know what's good for you!) After an hour, the pupils who make up the jury give their verdict. Willy is guilty of being a bad father and a bad husband. The lesson ends. It's been a very successful lesson.

What was your learning objective? The purpose of the trial activity was to show that *both prosecution and defence could make a case* (there wasn't much point in the trial otherwise). You want pupils to see that the text is complex and subtle and that texts are susceptible to interpretations by readers, audiences, actors, directors. We can see Willy as villain or as victim. So your next activity must take this point from the trial and make it explicitly so that pupils don't simply decide that Willy is now proven to be guilty man. That's not what they've learned. What they've learned is that you could see him as either, or as both, or as something else entirely, as long as you have text-based arguments for your view. You must at least talk about this: preferably, you must look at the matter of opposing interpretations in other places (contrasting film clips, not necessarily of the relevant text, but showing the same text interpreted in different ways; or, more easily, differing pupil opinions of right-and-wrong in a current *EastEnders* plot, or in real-life arguments).

So, serious points are made in this recreative work – points directly connected to examination or coursework preparation. The very structure of the trial mirrors the structure of formal discursive writing and is a powerful preparation and reference point for it – the ordering of arguments, the movement towards a conclusion, the use of supporting quotation.

In connection with this centrality of interpreting rather than merely understanding texts is the simple activity of orchestrating pupil opinion. Good questions to ask include imaginative projections – what would Slim say after the events of the book? – and occasional stock taking recaps – what was, *in your opinion*:

- the worst thing that Lennie did?
- the worst thing that was done to Lennie?
- a better way out of it?
- the moment when you knew for sure it wouldn't work?
- the saddest moment?

Simple jotting followed by discussion around questions like this, as you read or at the end, keeps the book alive.

A simple structure like the moral dartboard generates vibrant discussion of texts. Don't underestimate the power of a graphical focus like this compared to simply introducing a discussion topic. Individually, pupils sketch the dartboard and place the characters on it, the most blameworthy (or the least) at the centre, the others ranged outwards. You draw a large dartboard at the front of the room and pupils come to the front and place characters, giving reasons. Vigorous dispute ensues. This lesson works with texts at every secondary level, certainly including post-16. Some of my sixth-formers put Cordelia in the outer reaches of blame; some put her right at the centre. The discussion is exciting. What matters isn't who's right, but that nobody's right.

Of course, when pupils argue such opinions, they are keen to win; thus, they are keen to find strong supporting material. These are predominantly speaking-and-listening activities, but they're laying strong foundations for essay structures, the martialling of arguments, the use of relevant quotation. You are never away from exam preparation, so long as you remember these relevancies and point them out explicitly to pupils. When they write a formal essay, remind them of how they used evidence in a trial or a dartboard discussion. Good teachers do good activities but brilliant teachers make these connections. As we said in Chapter 2, it's the transition points that matter most.

There is a host of other activities – one character talks about another; one character says, "The one thing I shouldn't have done is . . ."; we write a better ending and compare them; we write one further chapter; we re-write an episode from a different viewpoint (e.g. changing from one character's perceptions to another's, or changing to third-person narration); we transform the mood of a description from optimistic to pessimistic; we draw (for example, the opening descriptions of *Of Mice and Men*); we make publicity material for the film-of-the-book. In all these cases we must be clear about two things: why we are doing it, and how this will link to subsequent activities in order to make that point. Properly deployed, such variety enhances the formal study of the text, supporting and developing understanding and the confidence that is essential to examination performance and, more importantly, to pleasure in reading.

Chapter 9

Drama

Mandie Wright

"We're going to do a bit of drama today; we're going to work in groups . . ." This statement, even if offered with coy optimism, will result in chaos. It is a signal for mayhem rather than a clear instruction. And yet often it's how a drama lesson begins. It's not so much off on the wrong foot as completely the wrong direction. What is this thing "drama" that you can just do a "bit" of it? Can you try it out and then abandon it if you don't get on? Why is it something attached to someone else's *real* curriculum like an encumbrance? Has it no independent validity of its own?

Well, yes. It has. In fact, in my opinion, it is one of the most useful and purposeful subjects on offer and one which can have the most profound and long-lasting positive effect influencing not only other branches of learning but the ability *to learn* itself.

So let's start that again . . .

The proposal

"Right, we're going to do a bit of drama today. We're going to work in groups on an idea and at the end we'll have a look and see how everyone's got on."

The sub-text

"Right, we're going to do *a bit*"

(so this is dabbling with something; it's probably optional)

"of *drama*"

(the term itself has indeterminate status; it may be difficult or threatening; the vagueness implies incredible freedom)

"today. We're going to work in *groups*"

(offered too soon, this is a signal for disarray; all I'm now concerned about is who I can trust not to dump me in embarrassment and how to avoid working with everyone else)

"on an idea and *at the end*"

(so this is the point of the session – it's not the journey but the arrival that counts)

"we'll have a *look*"

(so I was right in anticipating public exposure; everyone *will* be staring at me)

"and *see how everyone's got on.*"

(and there will be public judgment of my achievement – or lack of it).
   How could any students want to put themselves through this?

I used to start like this. I felt uncertain myself as to how this subject fitted the curriculum, seeming to be an adjunct to English along with the obligatory weekly drool round the library. Discussion with other staff centred only on *performance*, often the school play, and yet there seemed to be so much more to do with discovery and exploration behind the scenes.
   The freedom of drama can be terrifying or exciting. A brilliant drama teacher will be one who takes creative risks, borrowing from the world of the theatre, in order to achieve a spontaneous reality in the work of students. Acting should mirror life: life is spontaneous. We don't get the chance of a rehearsal; we *react* to the situations in which we find ourselves and the people we meet and conversations we have with them. If the purpose of the drama session is to:

* allow us to explore our own real-life interactions and those of others;
* explore the actions and motivations of characters in texts allowing ourselves to identify more fully with them and their situations;

- liberate the imagination and develop skills that will help us be more effective in its creative expression;

then all of these will be enhanced by an element of spontaneity in our sessions rather than too heavy reliance on pre-programming and attempts to say the right thing. We should be free to:

Speak what we feel, not what we ought to say.

And to a large extent this depends on the relative enjoyment being experienced by the teacher. Workshop leading is a high energy exercise and much of what happens in the room is affected by a form of sensory osmosis; after all, body language, status, nuance in the tenor or timbre of the voice are all the stuff of the sessions, the body of learning of the subject, so we should expect and encourage students to be observant of these. Hiding our own, then, is a non-starter. But this shouldn't be alarming or too daunting: it's an opportunity to relax and be creative with a strong sense of purpose. The essentials of this work are playfulness and acceptance, which must be present for the freedom that liberates creativity.

So far, so good; but how do these loose liberal words operate within an educational framework where control and organisation take precedence? Acting is a discipline. It requires physical fitness and muscular control, flexibility, adaptability, mental agility, stamina, tolerance, reciprocity . . . and that's without touching on the verbal abilities. Far from "dossing around", it is a mental and physical workout: indeed many actors start their days in the gym to be ready for rehearsal. And the greatest inhibitor to success is tension – physical or psychological. So the journey is towards release through self-discipline and in order to achieve that a whole new set of rules needs to be established in the working environment. The teacher needs to achieve a blend of fun, humour and playfulness with an evidently serious dedication to the purpose of the session. This as we'll see will bring commitment from the students and give you a strategy for ironing out discipline issues along the way.

Let's return to our opening question: "What is this thing 'Drama'?"

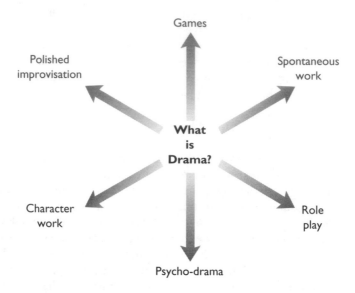

Games

These can form the basis of your work. These are the exercises that encourage self-awareness, exploration and self-development. They can be used to develop a specific range of skills such as observation, memory, focus and co-operation. They inevitably have the spin-off of group bonding and socialisation and, as a result of this, at the far end of the spectrum, are used as forms of therapy.

Character work

Here I'm referring to work based on adopting a named character who pre-exists in a text. The character has a given set of characteristics and the actor's job is to inhabit this character. This is, naturally, the stuff of most textual performance. It is, therefore, distinct from . . .

Role play

This is about situation. This is the stuff popular with industry, where companies employ drama workers to practise staff approaches to difficult situations, challenging customers, and so on. It's very useful for students also to experiment with alternative approaches to school, family or social situations, for example to test out interview technique. The distinguishing factor is that you as the actor remain yourself: it is the situation that alters.

Polished improvisation

I use the word "polished" here because I frequently find that the word improvisation on its own has two quite distinct meanings in the worlds of education and the theatre. This is the one generally meant by teachers. It is where students have had a chance to work in groups in order to present something. They may be exploring all kinds of ideas, attitudes or themes but the key is they have prepared their piece: it has a planned shape.

Spontaneous work

This is what improvisation means in the theatre. Whilst it may explore any of the same ideas as polished improvisation, the work is entirely spontaneous and unplanned. No-one knows what may happen. That phrase is enough to demonstrate why this is less popular in schools. There is more risk: but also there is more reward. A loss of inhibition is essential to creative freedom. If students are operating in a secure atmosphere where they are encouraged to take risks and where failure is something shared and discussed as part of a group process, far more exciting things can and will happen. The young mind is full of creative fertility – give it the chance to surprise you.

Psycho-drama

This uses the techniques of drama to explore the workings of the mind and personality. It has qualities of psychological introspection and may deal with primitive instincts and emotional exposure. For these reasons I feel it is best left in the hands of specialists. We are fragile beings and should be handled with care.

How to begin

New rules

Really it's about creating a new working environment. Drama works in an open space (if you're lucky!). It has the freedom of a sports hall, but without the demarcated tramlines. So here are a few tips to start with.

Tips for sessions

Establish conventions

Do this early, preferably in the *first session*. Students may well be a little intimidated by the space and what it might ask of them so make use of this. Leave it to the second session and it will be much harder.

Most useful are starting and ending conventions. It may seem obvious, but you will need not only time at the beginning to set up the session but maybe time at the end to confirm what's been achieved and/or to adjust the mood of the group before inflicting them on another colleague – not sending out fizzy bottles of pop. Defining the space, giving the session a shape, such as *starting and ending every session in a circle*, sends all the right subliminal messages. It's a self-disciplining convention: it signals that you want to be part of something, that all are equal and have a contribution to make, and that the session is ready to begin when everyone has had a moment to leave the trappings of other classwork (both physical – bags/shoes at the side, and mental – the off-loading of a struggle with a maths problem or an issue elsewhere in school) outside the circle.

This off-loading process is very important. The approach to drama can appear to work at variance to much other school work. Stand up straight/take your hands out of your pockets/speak properly/now *act*. It's not going to work is it? Yet it must be clear that your expectations are as high (if not higher, as they depend on *self-regulation*) as in other areas. So it's worth taking some time to explain how this will work and allowing that opening circle to monitor and if necessary re-establish conventions.

Talking about expectations is important too. Elsewhere in school there is much to do with judgment and anticipated success. Here there *must* be failure. No-one will be prepared to take risks if failure is something to be afraid of. Right from the outset, failure must be

seen as an inevitable and important part of the process that experimentation brings. If something doesn't work then that is part of the development of an idea and it will be interesting to discuss why and how it might be changed.

Agree a visual signal

You might want to change direction in mid-process when everyone is actively engaged. Some agreed way to signal to stop or give attention will be very useful. It can of course be something that's fun.

Similarly you might want an agreed signal for students to show when their idea or exercise is done. It can be difficult in a full room to distinguish between students who are still improvising and those who have moved on to a busy chat. Simply sitting, or moving to a given position, will cue you in.

Number round

Establishing from the outset a system where in a circle students call out in turn a defined sequence such as *123 123 123* or *apples pears oranges apples pears* . . . achieves efficiently an allocation for everyone. You know that if you walk round the circle allocating every individual yourself those behind you lose interest and forget what you gave them: speaking it aloud themselves is quicker, gives each student his own responsibility and makes them remember. It also allows you to:

- see at a glance if there is an even number of "apples";
- see where certain allocations have fallen if there are individuals you are wanting to involve more (or less);
- change difficult groupings. As friends will tend to stand together this system allows for *easy separation* by dividing them up (for example by saying, "all the 3's work over there").

Keep changing groupings

Students readily become insecure if they are accustomed only to working with particular friends. If from the outset the norm is to change frequently, fewer problems will arise. So use the system above to mix things round, try suggesting partnership with someone you haven't worked with yet today, suggest each pair contains a blue-eyed and a brown-eyed person . . . be ingenious and keep it fun! But to be successful you *must* introduce this right from the beginning before the practice of friend selection and comfort zones has set in.

Be sensitive to mood and atmosphere

Gauge if the group needs warming up or calming down – and know when to quit. Sometimes the best idea you've had, that you were really looking forward to using, will need to be abandoned or rested because something that happened before the class, or even the weather, has set the prevailing mood at variance to the exercise. Don't flog it. Return to it at the right time.

If an extra control system would be useful, a talking-stick or stone can be used, like the conch in *Lord of the Flies*. Only the holder of the item can make a contribution. It must be replaced at the centre of the circle *not* screamed for or passed on to friends.

Don't always "show" work

This is an important lesson in the value of process not product (see later under *Towards improvisation*).

Don't mix practical work and administration

Nothing is better designed to kill a session stone dead than to begin with a read-out of messages about assemblies/school trips/other staff's deadlines and so on, all of which will occasion questions and possibly anxieties that are not to do with the session. You have therefore not set the tone for the session but introduced a whole set of other preoccupations, which you are then immediately going to expect students to pack away and not think about until your session is over. If you have successfully installed *conventions* there will be no difficulty integrating this extraneous information at a later point of your choosing, where it will not intrude. It may well be useful to have an administration moment at the end of sessions anyway in order to programme any preparation you might need for the next.

Tips for you personally

Success in this work comes through confidence. Not the kind of confidence that is a mix of bravado and adrenalin that might get you through stage-fright, but the kind of personal stillness that makes space in the room, generates activity without feeling frenetic and underpins work with a sense of shared progress. It will allow you to be adaptable, responsive, sensitive, change direction, follow an unexpected new route, and so on. This comes from being secure with the work.

And it's catching.

If *you* have *confidence* in your methods this gives *security* to the group. This in turn generates *creative freedom*. Put simply, this work involves a great deal of trust. Any lack of conviction will be sensed and students need to feel in safe hands. The work must be playful and experimental: to play freely you must feel able to take risks without fear of judgment or uncomfortable laughter and this demands a feeling of equality. We're all in the same boat: we all resist making fools of ourselves; but we'll all risk it if the result is a positive and shared experience. A task "failing" in terms of performance or result might produce the most interesting discussion and follow-up work of the week.

Know what you're doing . . . but allow for discovery

Security in the work will come from knowing your *purpose*. You should never be in any doubt about this and it should be carefully and strategically integrated into your session's sequence. However, you might want to consider carefully how to do this. In some practical tasks it would be ludicrous to set out without a clear understanding of your aim and an impression of how you are going to achieve it – for example, pressing a pedal in a car and finding out by doing so that it was the accelerator. In artistic work, however, the creative urge can actually be suppressed by too deliberate an explanation of the process – for example, telling someone: "You are going to stand up and make everyone laugh by saying something extremely amusing . . ."

So sometimes students *not* knowing the purpose in advance may be vital for success. The precise outcome may be uncertain although the certainty is that there *will be* an outcome and learning will have taken place in the creative process. Too much instruction beforehand can kill the discovery and suppress the possibility of ideas you may not have foreseen. Consolidation after discovery can increase the feeling of achievement and satisfaction – you mean I had that much fun *and* learned all those things!

Don't think too hard about it

Sometimes the mind needs deflecting or occupying elsewhere in order to avoid self-consciousness, so an actor might rehearse Shakespeare running, jostling, throwing a ball to avoid over-cerebral concentration and to discover a fresh energy in the words. This equates to a form of sleight of hand: you are deflecting the conscious attention from the main event, allowing for instinctive and visceral connection. It also deals with *fear of failure* when approaching demanding work – no-one's judging you, they appear to be focusing on something else entirely.

Self-awareness good: self-consciousness bad

There is no way that a director can more effectively ruin an actor's performance than to identify a good moment in a production and comment on exactly which line they are doing well. They will never be able to say it the same again.

An actor is *aware* of himself in the space and can respond and make adjustments in the moment; if he becomes *conscious* of himself he may separate himself from the part, monitor his performance and start to think about what to do with his hands. As he approaches the line which received special mention he will not be a character speaking his thoughts for the first time but an actor trying to emulate a moment of perfection.

Above all, try to work in a way that is good-humoured and non-confrontational. Start with a new group to work in safe parameters, always allow for an escape route which doesn't compromise the task and where no-one loses face. Feel their anxiety . . . and *be sympathetic, encouraging and PLAYFUL!*

So to summarise:

Guideline principles

Confidence

Be brave enough to take risks yourself. You are asking for co-operation and acceptance from your group: remember this applies to you as well. Take a moment to ask – maybe audibly – is that going to work? – before dismissing a new idea raised by a student that doesn't appear to conform to your initial plan. Encourage the group to move towards a new responsibility.

Clarity

Think through how you will present work – how to explain, divide groups and so on. Plan your sequence carefully so that it builds upon earlier exercises. Keep up the momentum – if it flags they may feel silly or become hostile. This is high energy work for the workshop leader.

Sense of purpose

Keep clear in your mind *why* you are doing this – for example, the fact that everyone contributes may be more important than the quality of the contribution.

Good humour

Always remember how demanding and revealing what you are asking for is. Be honest – with your own failure and theirs.

And a note on discipline

It is the understandable preoccupation: all that space and creative freedom can be a heady mix. What I feel is of prime importance is to keep any discipline issues quite separate from the work. Stop to shout at someone taking advantage and the atmosphere will change for *everyone*.

- *Don't you dare behave like that . . .* (restriction and constraint)
- *Now, I want you to imagine that you're . . .* (liberation)

There's an immediate conflict.

This is not to say misbehaviour should be ignored. But consider the *reason* behind what's happening. There is bound to be an element of self-consciousness in this work and not everyone will feel comfortable that this is their strongest subject. Remember how you felt when teams were being picked for sport and you were standing waiting to be chosen, or when the maths test results were being read out in descending order and yours hadn't come up yet. There is no escaping that live work brings with it the fear of this kind of exposure. But this doesn't need to bring with it a feeling of victimisation. It all depends on getting right the principles above. Remember that students may well be at an age when they need to be liked and what their peers think of them and their image is very important – when is it not?

If a piece of work clearly had no effort behind it – talk about *this*. Distinguish the lack of effort from the lack of success in the piece. Try not to patronise or tell off; rather show how seriously you are committed to the nature of what they're doing – whilst keeping your cool and relegating attention-seeking behaviour to insignificance. This combination of serious approach to the work and good humour will help make people more comfortable with the whole feeling of exposure.

This is the kind of thing I mean:

Contrast:

> *I think that was just you being silly there – you weren't really trying . . .*

with

> *I can see you're finding this difficult – don't worry it's natural to hide behind laughter at first . . .*

The first is fairly certain to lead to protests and self-defence in the "Yes I was trying and I don't want to do this any more" style. The second:

- appears friendly and understanding – it's non-confrontational and you're not wound up;
- offers sympathy and support; and also, significantly,
- implies that if you do this again you're exhibiting your own fear of the task in trying to look big when you are really frightened of looking small.

Make any difficulties shared and remember you can't get anyone to act by shouting at them.

Getting into practicalities

Maybe you already run sessions in a way that is not based on preparing an "improvisation" in groups and then performing it – or at least if this is what you do and it is becoming repetitive maybe you are looking for a way out of this into new variety. The catch with drama based on the "prepare an improvisation" method is that:

- it provides the ultimate in exposure (remember "at the end we'll have a look and see . . .");
- it is extraordinarily demanding.

Because, as we said at the beginning, it's not really true spontaneous improvisation, you are asking for inspiration, refining, structuring and performing. From a student's perspective the pressure is like the over-dedicated approach to coursework – endless refining and refining and it's *never* as good as you wanted it to be; in fact by the end it's actually lost some of its initial impetus. But you tried *so* hard.

So the way to work is in a shared creative exploration. This happens best in circles. It's no accident that we identified these earlier as the best starting and ending shape: they are intrinsically egalitarian – and everyone can see everyone else at a glance. So aim for work beginning in a circle, encouraging everyone to participate, to develop ideas and share the weight of the exercise.

This kind of work may be all you do for weeks – maybe a term – until the atmosphere is one of laughter and trust and a group is entirely comfortable and confident with this approach to spontaneity and ready for any new challenge you may throw at them. What follows below is not a list of useful exercises – there are books full of these available some of which are listed in the Bibliography. There are many games that target particular skills; I have given some indications of these although in all cases *you* will decide the purpose. But the trick is *how* to use them, so rather than reproducing a new list I've given examples to demonstrate likely dilemmas, solutions and achievement aims.

If you are unfamiliar with any games or exercises mentioned, simple rules are appended to this chapter.

Warm-ups

Warm-up is a misnomer often resulting in the witty cry *I'm warm enough already* . . . It may be a physical necessity, to limber up bodies stiff from desk-sitting ready for demanding work but for less sophisticated groups it is more likely a way of creating the atmosphere and mood appropriate for the task ahead. However brief, some form of warm-up makes a difference to the engagement with the session's work, allowing a few moments of physical and mental preparation. You'll recognise the need to respond to the way the group enter the room and modify accordingly: too bubbly and they'll need calming and focusing; too weary and they'll need energising.

For physical release and control at the start of a session try silent screams – where you gather up your body and on a count of three give the largest scream involving the whole of your body *but making no sound at all* – similarly, whole-body yawns. These are quite liberating after a lot of sat-at-a-desk-tension. Don't underestimate however the simple release of shoulder shrugs (holding your shoulders tense and high behind your ears for a count of three then releasing them and dropping your arms, letting them swing loosely) and other arm-swinging or simple breathing exercises, for example, a simple breast-stroke movement breathing in through the nose and out through the mouth.

To combine release and tension, playground games such as *Cat + Mouse/Guards at the gate/Grandmother's footsteps* are useful. To energise, try *Knee fights*; and *Wizard/Witch/Goblin* or *Pig/Wolf/Farmer* (a physical version of the familar *Scissors/Paper/Stone*) work well. *Fruit salad* is useful as it can move a group from high energy release into more thoughtful truth-telling in the form of *Red shoes*.

For relaxation, note that when asked to relax a hand the first thing you will probably instinctively do is move that hand – in other words, you use the muscle. This is partly your mind identifying where that part of the body is – it is being involved in the process and making a deliberate action occasioning an increase in tension first. Remember how good you feel after vigorous exercise – and how relaxed. Students lying on the floor while you talk through a sequence of muscles throughout the body, each being tensed and then relaxed completely in turn, can have a calming, relaxing effect on the body. If it's the mind that needs releasing, *Guided fantasy* can also work extremely well and have a most positive effect.

Physical exercises are often the hardest, drawing attention to our sense of embarrassment with our bodies, our lack of elegant co-ordination. Remember how everyone stands apart at the beginning of parties and how we dim the lights and take a drink in order to overcome this? We are becoming less inhibited as a culture about this and rappers and TV fame programmes have made it all a bit more "cool", but you need to have strategies to release this self-consciousness and possibly to avoid the masquerade of "showing off" to hide embarrassment. Occupy the mind elsewhere and give the action a *purpose*. For example, don't say "Shake out your arms" (which personally makes me feel really silly) but "wave to a friend/shake out the tablecloth/froth up the bubbles in the bath" which give the mind a picture to think about and a setting to create in which the action *feels* appropriate.

In building physical conviction the graduation is always from the literal to the abstract. To mime moving a chair you should move a real one first to remind yourself of the shape, weight and necessary muscular action. You might start a group building a sculpture one figure at a time by:

- giving it a title before the start and having a group of sculptors construct and organise the figures to suit;
- allowing each figure to add *itself* one at a time and for the group to retitle the artwork as it progresses and changes, becoming something new;
- asking for movement so the piece becomes a moving machine that has a purpose at the outset, such as a machine to make bicycles;
- asking for the machine to reflect an abstract, such as machine of power, suspicion and so on;

- asking for a machine that reflects a text, such as a machine of *An Inspector Calls*.

Simple physicality can be encouraged by experimenting with mundane tasks. Ask someone, for example, to come into the room and sit down on a chair. Talk about each of us having a different energy level and pulse. Ask the class to observe and describe anything they can read into the body language and movement of this person. Ask for the entrance to be repeated giving different levels of urgency drawn from a situation. You are coming into a dentist's waiting room prior to a tooth extraction. You are coming in to your own room at the end of a very long day. How much can you read from the way someone moves, doing something so simple? Can it be done entirely neutrally?

What happens when someone can't do what you've asked and how do you prevent this swiftly turning into hostility?

A culture of acceptance is the key

The most important purpose to achieve is to establish that there is no right and wrong as long as there is commitment to the task. So you need always to keep clearly in mind what the true purpose *for you* the teacher is in the task you have set. This may not always be the same as the apparent goal and rule by which the game is being played. You must be ready to be flexible and think quickly. Imagine you are playing an early name game with a relatively unfamiliar group. The apparent goal is to remember names and information. Everyone in the circle in turn says their name and something which is true about them (*I had an egg for breakfast/I love dogs/I'm tired* etc.). When that is complete you take one person by the hand into the centre and introduce them to the group saying *This is . . . and he/she . . .* repeating both the name and the information they gave. This continues with each group member introducing another until everyone has had a turn. Now sooner or later someone will be unable to remember either a name or the detail attached to it. The game's rule appears to be to remember the names and information and demonstrate this individually in sequence – BUT *it's not a test!* What really matters? That everyone becomes confidently familiarised with each other and is left with a feeling that this is a friendly supportive group. Below this is an important, underlying message that to step alone into the centre of this circle is not threatening and this will be vital to encourage free volunteering at a later stage. So that is your agenda. And this colours your approach to the game. As soon as someone in the centre looks awkward you help them out; you ask those who haven't been introduced yet to indicate and ask the anxious player to *go over to someone you'd like to remember and ask for their name again – introduce her to us and we'll see if we can remember what she told us* . . . Or ask the person being introduced to prompt the person introducing. Notice they must not introduce themselves; the task must be completed by the right player even if it's all just repeated.

And this is all done with a light touch at fair speed and with much laughter. So what actually mattered was that the names were shared no matter by whom and the atmosphere was positive. It will have set the tone for much to follow.

A similar technique applies when playing *Pass the basket*. Here you may also be applying the "allow for discovery" principle. Don't tell all; don't become predictable. The apparent goal appears to be precise mime. You start with an imaginary basket before you. You mime removing something from your person and putting it in the basket. You pass it on. Each person in turn round the circle does the same. So far so good, and as with the name sharing you could stop there at the end of the first phase. But far more interesting is then to pass the "basket" round again with each of you in turn searching the basket for something you'd like, removing it, placing it on your own body and, making eye contact with the person who put it in, saying "Thank you" to them. Now, as the basket moves round and the more memorable things have gone, you will have to help. Again, think of it as shared experience not as a test – never leave awkwardness hanging in the air long enough to become real embarrassment. *Who put in something that hasn't been taken? Give us a clue* . . . etc. At the end you may notice that in fact several versions of one item may have been taken and one or two items forgotten altogether. Does it matter? It is up to you and the group whether you choose to point this out. But *your agenda* was quite complex here: you established the principle that everyone participates no matter what. And they *can*, with confidence, because *it is the participating that matters* at this stage far more than the content. You are establishing the rule that everyone joins in, everyone contributes, at their own level. The level will change, people will have different strengths, but being part of the activity is absolute; they are learning to take a risk and you are supplying a safety net.

The demand is not unfair – *we didn't know we had to remember* – that's true, you didn't spell out the second "memory" part of the game; if you had done, the first part would have degenerated into endless repetition of objects in order to avoid being caught out. But isn't an upgrade of skills – attention, observation, memory, etc. – the point of *all* classes? Isn't it better *not* to know when to prepare, in order to encourage alertness *at all times*? You are encouraging a mild air of unpredictability to kindle a creative spark. *As long as there is never a penalty*, for you cannot catch people out for something you haven't told them to prepare, this is an engaging and challenging way to work. You must be supportive and keep the whole thing light and enjoyable. It's the difference between a gentle affectionate teasing challenge and a full-blown practical joke with unpleasant consequences. *Be gentle.*

Trying to encourage students to work instinctively is demanding but worthwhile. It won't happen overnight. Whilst in the area of circles and principles, here's a word on *Pass the sound / movement*. Again, standing in a circle, you turn to face the person beside you and start making a sound, which you repeat over and over. The person you are facing joins in with the sound until you feel it is identical and simultaneous with the one you are producing. You release the person by turning back to face circle-centre. The second person turns towards person three and as he does so morphs his sound into a new one. This is picked up and copied by person three and so on. In a second round you can add the idea of movement to the sounds as well. You can play the game simply as a good teacher, everyone will have made some sounds and had a good time; but a brilliant teacher will ask for more. Don't feel that just getting a game to run successfully from one end to the other without disaster is enough. (Although there are days when it may feel like a miracle!) Show that you care about the quality of the work as you would in any subject . . . but keep the light touch. In this case you will have noticed that as the sounds were passed sometimes there were gaps as students turned to the next person as they "had to think" of what sound to make. Someone may even have stopped completely while they thought of what to do. Sometimes the sounds were overly contrived and "funny". So let the circle complete (don't stop and focus on someone), and then comment on where you saw this hesitation. Point out this is not failure but someone trying *too hard*, trying to make the "best" sound they can think of. Point out how ludicrous this really is – how can one sound be "better" than another? We don't need to impress each other; we need to respond to the task by letting go of the mental selection process and allowing an instinctive response; just letting it happen.

Sequencing your ideas deserves careful consideration. A workshop has a flow, an energy, a momentum. It should build: it should have a sense of progress and achievement in its fabric. It may be, for example, that a participant can gain a sense of satisfaction from the way the final exercise combines the skills experimented with earlier in the session. It is certainly likely that each exercise will last longer as the session runs in correlation to the amount of imaginative input required from the students. Short snappy games will combine to produce extended imaginative work.

Towards improvisation

Spontaneity comes from *Confidence*

The building blocks for improvisation are the knowledge and techniques developed in games and exercises.

Thinking on your feet will be essential. Three very useful exercises for this are *Bunny/Rabbit, Misnomer, and 123/clap23* – rules at the end of the chapter.

Allow experimentation and risk

A good teacher can organise a worthy session of polished improvisation. It may be structured around key themes, be well organised, have a moment of conflict and reach a conclusion. But it will have been carefully mapped out before the session and the outcome will be almost predicable. It will prove a point or demonstrate an issue. What it will not do is take a creative risk. A brilliant teacher will allow the students to enter into the reality of the situation in the moment. The responses will not be organised and the outcome will be utterly unpredictable. What this does is allow for genuine engagement with the conflict of these characters; genuine and unprepared dialogue; emotion which being unrehearsed is far likelier to speak of where the students are in their real contact with life and the world around them.

This doesn't mean this session is now unprepared. It will, in fact, take far more careful preparation and demand that you deploy some of the same skills you are expecting from your students. You will have to be flexible and quick-thinking to make on-the-spot responses. But the rewards will be far greater.

As we said earlier, far too much time in student group improvisation is spent in the planning and writing stage – what we called "polishing" – and very little time acting. In the end, this is a dynamic, "live" medium; students have plenty of time to write elsewhere. We don't expect actors to be writers and directors. By asking a group to prepare something for presentation, you are requiring a very sophisticated panoply of skills: imagination to create an idea, playwrighting to create character and shape story, script-writing to create interesting dialogue, directing to realise this with a sense of staging and awareness of audience . . . and the acting hasn't entered into it yet. It's an immense demand.

Break it down and make it manageable

Don't ask too much too soon. Break down the task and unlock the necessary skills to develop a group with the requisite flexibility to explore things spontaneously. This is not as hard as it sounds.

If a player is unable to take on playing a character and creating a situation: let him create the playing space *only* first. Ask him to enter and create the room for the audience. It could be an exam room, huge and cold; a small dark room where the bulb has gone and the only light is coming through the door; a cinema, and so on. For an inexperienced group, entering a room can be a guessing game. The group send someone out and then decide on a situation. The one outside is someone for whom they are waiting – the teacher of the group, a visiting speaker, a surgeon entering an operating theatre, the DJ for the party, and so on. The one outside enters and has to play along until he can fully participate in his role showing that he has realised who he is. He doesn't guess out loud; he joins in.

For a more experienced group, A can enter and establish the nature of the room and when ready call for B to whom he gives a feed line, which B must accept, cueing him in to the nature of who he is – for example *I need my assistant – Oh thank God here he is.*

The more sophisticated and practised the group the more players can enter this scenario, each establishing their own identity and then introducing the need for a further player. Encourage some conflict in the interaction.

One of the session "tips" earlier was don't always show the work. *Improvisation does not always need to be watched.* It is a process of creative exploration. Accustom a group to improvising freely and enjoying the process without becoming concerned about an end product. Of course you, as session leader, will be monitoring all that is happening but there should never be an inevitable sense of having to *show* what has been done. It will, after all, never be the same again.

What is, however, very useful is to adopt a freeze and pointer technique. Habituate a group to this as a working practice from the early stages. Whenever working, they should know that if asked to freeze they hold their current position and attitude still and in silence. What you are adding is the pointer which can activate any moment you choose. Say you have a group working in pairs. They freeze. You move round the room clicking your fingers to select and point at one pair. This pair then immediately springs into life continuing what they were doing. As soon as you click and select another pair the first freezes. In this way you can activate a selection of work. But no-one will ever know who's next or expect it to be them. It never (or rarely) includes everyone. The advantages are:

- It's unfinished: there is no sense of *ours isn't good enough* as this obviously isn't a "final performance";
- It's unpredictable: no-one has a chance to discuss or worry about how to improve or change what they've been doing because it's about to be seen;
- It's not definitive or "the best": you can vary who you choose to make sure it appears random whilst ensuring you share interesting or alternative approaches. It is important these selections are very brief. I sometimes call them eavesdropping.

Unlocking imagination

At the beginning of this section I identified three good exercises to encourage quick thinking. You might also play *Word association* and *Word dissociation*. Both will continue the theme of liberated thought, not vetted or "improved". Instinct leads us to check if the thought is "clever" enough before saying it. Avoid allowing any comment between individual words to avoid this inhibition and stop and request an alternative any time you sense too much "wit" entering and showing conscious decision. Earlier games such as *Pass the sound/movement* have paved the way for this. If you are aiming this piece of work towards a particular text it is of course also possible not to play "fair" yourself. Your words may be carefully selected to trigger a chain of thought connected to the themes of the text you are about to read. For *A Midsummer Night's Dream* you might offer *love fear wood trees sex* for example, to see what images arise.

Blocking

You want to move a group towards sharing responsibility for the progress of a workshop just as a cast would take responsibility for a staged performance. A common problem in improvisation is *blocking*, where a player rejects the imaginative proposal of another, refusing the situation suggested. I demonstrate this in workshops by playing "B" to an "A", who is told to start off an improvised situation and then feed me an entrance line such as *I think I can hear my mother coming.* I enter with something like *I'm not your mother. I'm Aunt Jemima come over to stay from Queensland.* The question raised is of course what strategy you adopt for this kind of situation. The reasons for blocking can be diverse. It looks obstructive; it might evidently spring from embarrassment; it might also be competitive: *I've got a better idea.* Be careful about simply blocking the blocking, reprimanding the player and telling them to play the game. This may simply escalate the situation especially if the blocking was "funny" and got a laugh. The same student will be tempted to try an even "grander" block the next time and gain further popularity. Again acknowledge the problem for what it is – and sometimes the creativity with which the offer has been deflected! Remember the earlier maxim of acceptance. There are two approaches to this situation. You would want to establish that the game is acceptance and whatever you are given you must go with it. This is of course your main aim. But sometimes it might be useful, if more appropriate to the mood, to acknowledge the humour created and turn it into an exercise in itself to get this urge out of the way.

Call it "blocking" to reinforce the term and set up situations where A improvises, throws a feed line that dictates character and situation to B (*It's my mother and she's really angry with me*) whose job is then to refuse it in an outrageous way. After a while a group can realise that this is limited in its entertainment and that while it may be funny, no situation ever develops or goes anywhere.

There are two simple games that should be played earlier to help establish these two different principles. If you have done this the group will have already absorbed the fundamental terminology. They are *Yes, and . . .* and *No, you didn't . . . .* Play *Yes, and . . .* early in your acquaintance with a group. In a circle you start a simple story-situation based on an invented shared memory. So you might begin: *Do you remember when we went to town to get something for John's birthday?* The next player round the circle *must* start their contribution with *Yes, and . . .* so, for example, *Yes, and you saw that watch you thought he'd like.* The next player continues: *Yes, and when we went in to get it you realised you'd left your money at home.* And so on, with each player taking on the same situation as it is passed to him and becoming one of the same two figures in the story so the first-person narrative is sustained as it passes on. The same technique can be used for straightforward third-person story but the *you* and *I* recall is more familiar to begin with. The significance is that *there can be no rebuttal* of the situation; the *Yes, and . . .* structure insists on agreement and hence acceptance. This again is one of your "hidden" agendas. There is no need to spell out that this is an acceptance game. The principle will be absorbed and can be referred back to in a later situation of blocking in improvisation almost in code – *No, this is a "Yes, and . . ." situation, accept it and move on.*

The other *No, you didn't* game demonstrates deliberate blocking and how it makes a story change direction. In a circle you begin with a statement such as *I went to the pictures the other day.* The next player round the circle blocks this, saying simply: *No, you didn't.* The *next* player, again adopting a shared persona, moves it on with *You're quite right I couldn't get in so I wandered round town till it was dark.* Next player: *No, you didn't.* Next player (still shared persona): *You're quite right, I . . .* and so on.

Psychology

Many teachers now play *Hot-seating.* This can be a successful exercise with the proviso that it should always be clear at what moment in the character's life the interview is taking place. For example, I cringe when I hear students announcing "After I died I thought . . ." not having clarified that this moment of exploration should be happening just *before* a character's untimely accident. This speaking from beyond the grave distances the reality of the situation, turning it into simply an academic exercise rather than a revelation of the character's psychology. Similarly, setting the interview just before a significant life-event might allow for interesting insights into the character's hopes and expectations without the benefit of hindsight.

A simple experiment with *Given circumstances* is very effective. As with physical exercises it is useful to play with reality first. You feed students lines which offer information about their past:

> Someone important to me when I was young was . . .

> For my sixth birthday I remember . . .

their present:

> People tend to think I'm . . .

> I like to think I'm . . .

and their future:

> What I'd like most next year . . .

> When I get home I'll wish I'd . . .

There are important rules to this game:

1 No-one may comment in between lines. They must simply be stated and left – *not* responded to.
2 Each student *must* repeat the beginning part of the line you offer making a *complete statement*. This is most important; if not adhered to the whole exercise will start to sound like any question-and-answer interview. You are encouraging people to volunteer their own piece of information.
3 For this to be possible, any level of response must be accepted. So someone may complete: *The most important thing to me at the moment* . . . with either *The most important thing to me at the moment is food*, or *The most important thing to me at the moment is to be accepted by this group*. Any level of engagement is fine; it is the player's choice how personal he/she chooses to be. Similarly you, of course, can offer a mixture of levels of leading lines.

Having established this game in "reality", it can also be angled towards a piece of text. The whole group as one take on a character. Each member of the group in turn makes a complete statement in response to the beginning that you feed; each voices his or her response in the voice of this shared group character. So again for *A Midsummer Night's Dream* you might start lines for the shared character of Hermia with:

- I've never left the city before because . . .
- I like to get my own way because . . .
- If I love someone I . . .
- If I really want something I keep . . ,
- I think my father is . . .

In the same way *Hot-seating* may be shared amongst a whole group if one person is reluctant to take the burden.

Psychology might also be explored by playing one scene in any number of ways. Take a simple moment from any text or create your own scenario or situation. Play it with no guidelines just to see what happens. Introduce the idea of *choice and decision* and allow the class, guided by you, to change what happens in the next replay simply by changing the prevailing mood or attitude of *one* character. This encourages students' ownership of the idea, continuing to discourage the feeling of there being a right answer, a right way to do this.

We have an obsession with story: maybe you have the vocabulary at your command – and stamina – to create a whole novel; maybe you don't. Maybe you have a small pot of paint and a whole room that could be decorated; your choice is to dilute the paint and cover the room in a way that will never be satisfying or rewarding – or to feel enriched by painting one wall in a glowing colour. You can cover the whole plot with little involvement or you can richly engage with a significant moment. Taking a key moment and using this as a way into a full text will work particularly well for complexity such as is found in Shakespeare. Much can be learned from true understanding of the psychological conflicts and agendas of one key moment. This then forms a springboard to predict a character's behaviour elsewhere in the play. Working on moments also helps with understanding the *right to fail* or *change your mind*. The ideas are still fluid; you have not yet made a total commitment to a view of whole piece.

Drama work of all kinds, then, is best delivered in the framework of a shared experience; an explorative process where ideas are not over-defined but remain flexible and open to interpretation, where commitment and sincerity are absolute but playfulness and experiment are essential, and where the principles of risk and spontaneity encourage imaginative freedom.

Appendix: rules for games and exercises

Cat and Mouse

One player designated cat, another mouse. Cat chases mouse. Two different approaches:

1   Other players form a grid holding hands in rows of parallel lines. Cat and mouse let loose to run up and down grid. At strategic moments workshop leader shouts "change!" and all drop hands and turn a right angle to join up to form another grid (facing a side wall).
2   Other players link arms in pairs. Cat and mouse chase until mouse links arms with any one of the pairs. This "bumps" the other member of the pair off to become a new mouse.

Guards at the gate

Group divides into prisoners and guards. Again two different approaches:

1   Four guards stand in a row facing the prisoners. They would be just able to touch fingertips. All others line up in single file rows facing the gaps (the gates) between the guards. Guards close their eyes. Prisoners attempt to move silently between them, out of the gates. If a guard hears a sound he/she will raise their arm attempting to catch someone in the gateway. Anyone so caught is sent back to prison.
2   Guards stand round the edge of the circle, prisoners at the centre. Same process, trying to escape through the gaps.

Grandmother's footsteps

A surprising number of students have never played this as children. One "grandmother" stands with back to the rest of the group facing a wall. All others start at an opposing wall. The challenge is to touch grandmother on the back. She may turn round at any moment and anyone seen moving *at all* must return to the starting wall.

Knee fights

Players are in pairs. The challenge is to make three "hits" on the opponent's knee with your hand. As the same challenge applies to both of you, you will of course also have to use your hands to protect your own knees. Should you play fast and furious or strategic and slow?

Wizard/Witch/Goblin or Pig/Wolf/Farmer

Group divides into two opposing teams. The team decides secretly which of the three characters they want to be for the round. Agree in advance a gesture which denotes each character. As in *Scissors/Paper/Stone*, there is a circular order of rank: Wizard beats Witch beats Goblin beats Wizard/Farmer shoots Wolf eats Pig beguiles Farmer with curly tail!

Teams stand in two long facing lines some distance apart. Workshop leader counts '1–2–3!' as teams step three paces forward and then adopt the position/make the gesture. In a split second the groups assess which is dominant. The losers must run for the safety of touching their home wall. The winners must catch as many of them as they can before they reach safety. Anyone caught, joins the winning team. Play on, agreeing a character afresh.

Fruit salad

"Number round" using fruit, i.e., "apple pear banana apple pear . . ." and so forth. Mark places on a circle with one too few for all players (using a shoe is a simple way to do this) and put someone in the middle. The caller at the centre calls one of the fruit. All people of that fruit must swap places. The one at the centre will attempt to take one of their places on the circle leaving a new caller at the centre. At any point, he may call "fruit salad" and everyone must swap.

. . . and Red shoes

This game-play can then be adapted for a subtler game where the caller calls something which must be true for himself. This might be visual – "anyone wearing trainers" – or informational – "anyone who has a dog" – and can develop to be more abstract – "anyone who believes that . . ."

Guided fantasy

The group adopts a relaxed position on the floor, eyes closed. The workshop leader takes them through an experience via a series of questions. In order to do this you should have these ready in your mind; they should suggest scenery, experience and should be open to imaginative interpretation. For example, "You are standing outside. Is it warm or cold? Look into the distance – how far can you see? There is something you can just make out – a building of some sort . . . start to walk towards it." And so forth. Opening doors, boxes, gateways etc. is always good. Be careful to keep the questions/ suggestions open. At the end you might want to allow volunteers to share their stories/experiences. These may feel quite personal, students get quite deeply involved in this exercise, so I would never push this.

Bunny/rabbit

Players stand in a circle, one takes on the role of the pointer in the centre. The pointer points (quite fiercely) at a group member saying "bunny". The one pointed at must adopt the position of bunny – little raised paws and buck-teeth – while the ears are supplied by a raised hand from each of the two group members either side of the "bunny's" head. Do this continuously and quite fast. Occasionally introduce the command "rabbit" instead. At this, no-one should move at all. Any mistakes and the loser takes over in the centre.

Misnomer

Players stand in facing pairs. Keeping to a rhythm (keep reminding them of this as it will get forgotten) each in turn names and points to a part of the body, e.g. "This is my nose". As A points and names, B gives a single clap that punctuates the rhythm. B then names and A claps. So on in sequence. Then introduce lying. So A says "This is my nose" but points to his ear. B, instead of clapping, must correct, saying simply "Ear". Play continues, including lying and truthful naming, still aiming to keep to the rhythm.

123/clap23.

Again in facing pairs, players count alternately 1–2–3, 1–2–3, 1–2–3, and so forth, but as there are two of them the numbers will not immediately repeat. When this is running smoothly, and groups will vary tremendously in how easy or hard they find this, introduce something physical instead of one, so "clap–2–3". Continue and then substitute something, say a stamp of the foot, for 2, and then something for three.

Word association and word dissociation

For word association the leader starts by saying one word, the player next to him says the *first* thing that comes into his mind and so on in turn round the circle. This should be an instinctive response as unconsciously chosen as possible.

By contrast Word *dis*sociation is a conscious process. The sequence is the same but the word spoken must have absolutely no possible link with the word that went before it. Players can "buzz" in a challenge if they think they spot a link. This can be very useful as an imaginative release as players will quickly get the idea (if you introduce it by doing this yourself) of making quite abstract links and connections between words, weaving elaborate stories.

Hot-seating

A player takes a central seat *in character* and is interviewed by the rest of the group. As mentioned above, in the case of a fictional character it is important to establish at what point in their life this interview is taking place. It may be useful to try this with a person drawn from real life, present or historical, as practice first. It may also be useful to have time to prepare.

Chapter 10

Differentiation

Conscientious English teachers feel guilty most of the time. The job is never finished to perfection, the demands can never be fully met; schools are places of permanent compromise; and nowhere is this anxiety more pronounced than in the business of differentiation. It's a matter of common sense that efficient teaching takes account of the varying personalities of those who are learning, but in practical and realistic terms, what are you meant to do? You have twenty-eight pupils with twenty-eight reading ages, personal histories, individual needs, learning styles, interests, idiolects, SAT scores, attitudes and preferences, and some of those have changed since last week. And you have four classes a day. They are all mixed-ability classes, because all classes are mixed-ability classes (children don't come in ability-batches of twenty-eight); and a good deal of differentiation isn't just about ability anyway. You need some straightforward and achievable answers to the many complex questions which differentiation asks. And eventually you need a life of your own.

Firstly, stop worrying about it – anxiety is counter-productive; and you are already differentiating a great deal in your teaching. Take stock of what you already do. For example, do you:

- *talk to individuals about their work* in any context? Do you discuss their coursework drafts with them? Do you work on their reading choices in the LRC?
- *always QDO?*
- *give some extra explanation*, perhaps during a QDO session when task-setting, or in response to a pupil question?
- *vary class questioning*, for example by avoiding YAVA?
- *give pupils time to discuss tasks in pairs*, perhaps as part of QDO?

- *write comments on children's work*, addressing its strengths, suggesting improvements and developments, and engaging with the content?
- *ask the class questions*, for example during a plenary, or a lesson transition?
- *answer pupil questions*, and make spaces for them to ask?
- *assess pupils' work*?
- *provide a variety of resources*?
- *use pupils as experts*, for example by allowing them to plan presentations on their own chosen areas of knowledge?
- *allow peer assessment* from time to time, so that pupils see (or hear) and discuss each other's work?
- *have group discussion*?
- *allow pupils to work in areas of personal interest*?
- *give a choice of tasks* from time to time; for example, allowing groups to choose their feedback method, or allowing individuals to choose their text type (poster, leaflet, newspaper letter)?
- *use a variety of activities* to move towards your learning objectives?
- *explain things two or three ways*?
- *set research homeworks*?
- *set "family" homeworks*, such as interviewing your mum about her attitudes to Shakespeare?
- *chat*?
- *praise*?
- *ask for pupil opinions* on an issue or a text, and perhaps list and discuss those opinions?
- *run interactive starters*?
- *work collaboratively with the whole class*, for example, on a shared writing exercise?
- *work with selected groups*, for example on shared reading?
- *do drama*?
- *work with learning support assistants*, including briefing and debriefing them?
- *work with computers*?
- *use an interactive whiteboard*, for example to note and print pupil contribution?
- *do pair work*?
- *evaluate learning and modify your teaching*?
- *encourage pupils to keep a reading/oral/English log*?

You will notice two things about this list. Firstly, although it's a list of differentiation routines, it's also a list of good classroom practices. Good teaching and differentiation are almost synonymous. The second thing is that you can answer "Yes" to many of these questions. You are already differentiating on a regular basis.

There are, of course, well-documented categories of differentiation – differentiation by task, by outcome, by resource, by support and by response – and these are partly covered by the list above. Differentiation by *outcome* was for years the English teacher's standby – all pupils will write different stories, even if given the same title – but this is a passive and inadequate approach. Setting a range of *tasks* where pupils choose or are directed to appropriate levels is more robust but, especially as it is likely to combine with the preparation of varied *resources*, this presents enormous practical difficulties to a working teacher with minimal preparation time. Differentiated *response* may happen spontaneously as you mark work or talk to pupils, but there's nothing particularly systematic about that, and indeed all of these approaches require analysis and careful monitoring. The rewards are great but the demands are significant.

It may be that, over a period of time and (ideally) working with other teachers you will prepare well-resourced and differentiated medium-term plans. You can find (for example) a range of versions of a common text like Dickens' *A Christmas Carol* which offers the original, several "re-tellings", a comic-strip version and a range of films; or you can create or find work cards to help with sentence-level grammar at varying levels of sophistication, and so on. As well as providing such materials, a plan needs to consider how they will be targeted and monitored. It's not unusual to see great efforts being made in resource creation undermined by quite crude classroom deployment in terms of who does what and why, often based solely on rough-and-ready notions of ability. You cannot create ambitious, differentiated and targeted work schemes overnight, and, for the sake of your personal sanity and survival, you should attempt this as a long-term project, focusing on one class at a time over a period of months or years, and working with colleagues to create central resources.

But in the meanwhile, there are more immediate, achievable and highly effective ways of extending your differentiation repertoire so that your pupils feel valued as individuals with their own access to the curriculum. Consider differentiation by *teacher language*, by *rotation*, by *choice* and by *multiple access*.

Teacher language

How are you making sure that all pupils, whatever their ability, their linguistic competence, their first language, are going to make sense of what you say? Key moments of teacher-talk – explanation and task-setting, for example – need to be presented and re-presented in a variety of alternative ways, using different tones, registers and examples drawn from a variety of contexts. You must plan more than one way of saying and showing key ideas. This is easy for English teachers, but it needs preparation. You need to use varied language including synonyms, similes, symbols, alternative explanations, ranges of examples and physical modelling if appropriate. Remember that, in explanations, an example is worth a thousand definitions.

Rotation

Another simple, uncumbersome approach is that of rotation; this is also available to you without massive planning and resource creation.

A couple of years ago I had three extremely able pupils in my A-level group. They were writing essays that could have been published in literary journals, and their conversation in class was extraordinarily analytical and detailed. Of course I was aware that they shouldn't be allowed to dominate the discussion, while at the same time it was clear that less able pupils were benefiting from listening to them. Striking that balance is part of differentiation, and any decent teacher will be thinking about it. In particular, I had to be sure that the three or four pupils who were aiming at D grades didn't feel intimidated, inhibited or undervalued, and that they took part in class activities. I did this by creating discussion activities with clear structure and focus, by judicially altering groupings, by creating tasks which allowed for differentiated responses, and by generating discreetly differentiated research tasks.

However, it became clear to me as I taught the class that a further group of pupils – four bright girls, who in most A-level classes would have been the predominant group – was suffering. They were interested but made little contribution to discussion, and this is vital, since moving the mouth exercises the brain; post-16 teaching is essentially discursive. I decided to focus on them for about three weeks. I required their inclusion in discussion and I focused my oral and written responses on them. There was a noticeable change in their participation and confidence, though I hope and believe that no one noticed what I was doing.

Differentiation is frightening because of its scale, and this is one simple way to bring it down to size. At any given time, you should be focused on a given sub-group, chosen not necessarily by ability (the girls at the back, the quiet boys, the ones who don't like the novel, the middle row). Members of this group receive the bulk of your spoken and written attention for a week or two, and then you move on. It's not so defined that anyone can notice it; it doesn't exclude others; but it forces you to spread yourself evenly, and it doesn't require you to try to be all things to everybody all the time. This group, which only exists in your mind, is questioned a little more than the others; its answers are responded to a little more than the others; it works with you on guided and shared work a little more than the others; it has its written work marked a little more thoroughly than the others; and then you move on.

Inclusion, not segregation

Differentiated teaching provides a multiplicity of access routes to the learning and you can achieve a great deal without graded worksheets and red and blue tables. Think of the learning as a carousel; the pupils climb on from their different points, at different speeds, in different ways. Howard Gardner's concept of *Multiple intelligences* is at its simplest a straightforward but very powerful way of dealing with this. Different children understand things in different ways, and the implication of Gardner's list is that we should generate variety in our teaching. We have already seen that variety is central to good English teaching, anyway. Gardner's original list is of eight intelligences (see Table 10.1). It is, however, possible to add to the list. For example,

Table 10.1 Multiple intelligence

Linguistic intelligence ("word smart"):
Logical-mathematical intelligence ("number/reasoning smart")
Spatial intelligence ("picture smart")
Bodily-kinesthetic intelligence ("body smart")
Musical intelligence ("music smart")
Interpersonal intelligence ("people smart")
Intrapersonal intelligence ("self smart")
Naturalist intelligence ("nature smart")

I've found that some pupils understand new ideas when they are set into a story (see *The car and the lorry*, below). You could call this *narrative intelligence.*

The point about multiple intelligences is not that you go into preparation overdrive creating eight or nine alternative sets of approaches and dividing the class into learning-style groups, but that you accept *one simple, basic principle* and plan that into your lesson. Consider the key, explicit learning moments; mark them on your plan; they may well occur in transitions; they will deal with the learning objectives. Decide *how you will deal with these key concepts in a variety of ways,* which will create a number of access routes. All pupils can deal with all of the alternative routes; they will work differently for different individuals; they will act as reinforcements of each other for everybody.

Multiple access is a natural extension of objectives-based planning. Let's consider an example. Your objective is that pupils, who are studying Shakespeare, will understand the iambic pentameter. A good teacher will pause and explain this metrical device when she thinks it's an appropriate moment but a brilliant teacher will decide that this is a significant piece of new learning, that it needs to become embedded and available for future use rather than being cursorily glanced at, and so that it deserves time and a range of approaches.

Consider your own personal preference for taking in new ideas; consider the ways in which you can understand iambic pentameter. Some people will hear it when you repeat a few lines of Shakespeare and point out the pattern. Some people will get hold of it when they beat it out on the desk with rulers as drumsticks. Some will count it – five accents, each containing a weak and a strong beat ($5 \times 2 = 10$). Some will value the definition of the words (iamb implies 2, pentameter means 5, the whole means a decasyllabic line of five iambs). Some will chant it, perhaps in groups, either in words or rhythmic sounds (*ti-tum-ti-tum-ti-tum-ti-tum-ti-tum*) Some will make up their own lines (*I think I'll go and have a cup of tea . . .*) Some will see it when you make a diagram of it on the board – ./././././ Some will like the heartbeat analogy. Some will want to compare it to ordinary speech.

There are at least eight different approaches listed above, all drawn from the experience of teaching, not from a need to fulfil Gardner's list, though you will see that they do conform to several of his intelligences. These activities work together in the classroom; *there's no need to segregate them, or the pupils;* they will settle after a time on the combination that makes most sense to them. The teacher focuses on a single clear objective, rather than "doing" the Shakespeare line-by-line, providing a rich and varied environment for learning around a clear content focus. For each child, one or two approaches will be central, others will enrich and confirm, others will echo; the combination of analysis and creativity will generate rounded, personal understanding.

The deployment of this range of approaches is a matter of judgment; you may not use them all; you don't have to stolidly work through a sequence of activities; some of these will be brief additional suggestions. *They will often be a matter of teacher language rather then of discrete activities.* You will monitor and evaluate the learning and call up these approaches as necessary until understanding is secure. The important thing is that you've selected your key objectives and made planning notes about the various access possibilities. This is really commonsense teaching, but it's surprising how often teachers don't seem to have alternative routes ready in the background. If a pupil says he doesn't understand, how are you going to rework the learning?

In the classroom, this will mean giving twenty minutes, not two, to the iambic pentameter; it will mean triangulating away from Shakespeare; it will also mean that your pupils have a chance of genuinely understanding (and so remembering) the concept.

There are always these alternative routes, and you need to devote a portion of planning time to them. Once you have them, your differentiated teaching will mean that you can move whole classes to higher levels of understanding. A Year 7 mixed-ability class will understand similes if you spend time on the simile lesson outlined in Chapter 2 because you have followed key planning precepts, such as combining analysis and creativity, and you have provided linguistic, visual and active routes, and so your planning has become differentiated. In teaching *dramatic irony* to a Year 10 class, you might

- discuss *EastEnders* plots;
- tell jokes;
- consider the text;
- make up your own dramatic irony plots for different genres – comedy, horror etc.;
- define it in terms of audience understanding and reaction;
- do dramatic-irony diagrams showing levels of understanding (see Chapter 8);

- do *The car and the lorry* (see below);
- do dramatic-irony predictions;
- define with reference to other types of irony;
- storyboard a dramatic-irony situation;
- find a television example for homework;
- look at some video examples – what do they have in common?

You are aiming at more than just a lot of examples; you're aiming at a range of learning opportunities that don't duplicate each other but allow different access routes. You are allowing for example a *graphic* understanding in the irony diagram, a *narrative* understanding in the car and the lorry (see below), a *language* understanding in the definitions, a *creative* understanding in the plot construction, a *research* understanding in the television work, and so on.

While it's certainly helpful for pupils to think about their own learning preferences, the point here isn't for you to decide on each pupil's learning style and aim certain approaches at him as a result; the point is to offer the variety to everyone; they will naturally fixate on the approaches that work for them. In any case, these learning preferences will change over time; and different approaches will suit different objectives for the same individual. I personally always find the dramatic-irony hierarchy diagram the quickest way to analyse a scene; in that area, I like the visual. But, when it comes to iambic pentameter, I hear the rhythm. A visual diagram is of no help to me there, I don't see the beats. So these two pieces of learning appeal to different styles within one individual.

The car and the lorry

I only have to say, "You remember dramatic irony?" for pupils to say, "Oh, yes, that's the car and the lorry." It's a stereotype film plot which I often use to introduce the concept.

A car is parked half-way down a mountain track, and a family from the car is picnicking on the track. Higher up the mountain, above several hairpin bends on the same road, a lorry is out of control. It is plunging down towards the innocent picnickers, who are a happy family with small children and clever pets. The film switches backwards and forwards from the car to the lorry. *When we look at the car, we think of the lorry; when we look at the lorry, we think of the car.* I draw the mountain track on the board, and we also do a knowledge hierarchy, thus

Audience

Car   Lorry

Or, if the lorry driver somehow knows about the car, which may add even more excitement:

Audience

Lorry

Car

Personal choices

We have a chance with differentiation when we stop allowing it to be an anxious, overwhelming grind and recognise it as a spur to a lively, enjoyable, varied, inclusive and active classroom. Perhaps we need to think of it as less of a science and more of an art, at least as creative as it is analytical.

We have mentioned *pupil choice* in every chapter, and this is one key to a pleasurable, differentiated classroom. It can occur at every level of transaction. It can inform the choice of materials to work on – they choose their own adverts, their own topics, their own media, their own products, their own leaflets. They choose whether to make audio tapes or write speeches about animal welfare. They choose whether to write a poem or something non-literary about old age. They choose whether to be for or against the necessity of war. Of course such choices need monitoring, and some children will tend towards easy or repetitive options, so you will need to guide them, but teachers are perfectly able to do that. There won't be choices in every lesson; and there will be generic objectives and structures to underpin the freedoms (see, for example, Chapter 7).

Individual reading sessions allow pupils to follow their interests, though they can be problematical. Pupils sitting doing silent reading for ten minutes at the start of the lesson is quite a common sight in today's classrooms, but there's an incongruity between the freedom of the choice of book and the regimentation of the reading itself. You must encourage personal reading, but perhaps compulsory silent sessions aren't the way to foster individuality. Certainly everybody seems to be relieved when they're over, including the teacher, and the follow-up is often fairly minimal. Personal reading is a personal matter, and perhaps the time and place of that reading is personal as well. If you need to monitor it, this can be done through reading logs or other generic activities, such as pupil-led book – recommendation sessions in the library.

I still have a toothbrush that was given to me by a Year 8 girl years ago because I answered a question correctly about dentistry. She had given a fifteen-minute talk to the class and had chosen dentistry because it was her brother's profession. Each member of the class (they could choose to work in pairs) gave one such "expert" talk every Friday through the year; they had a week to prepare them. One girl brought in her pony. One boy brought in his scrambler motorbike and drove it towards us up a near-vertical bank. I was frightened at the time, but not as frightened as I am now, when I wake up in the night thinking about it.

I also have a piece of work that my daughter did when she was in Year 9. She had no great love for history, but she became fascinated on a family holiday in France by some rough inscriptions made by prisoners on the stone walls of a ruined prison across the road from our hotel. She copied them out and took them home. They were the beginning of an entirely personal scheme of work which she called *Freedom* and for which she read and responded to, among other things, *A Tale of Two Cities* and Terry Waite's account of being held hostage, *Taken on Trust*. This was an impressive and sustained effort on her part, and it happened because her English teacher allowed her to follow an enthusiasm and provided support. Brilliant teachers seek out ways of making this possible at some point for everybody. They listen to pupils so that they know what they're capable of. It isn't so difficult to do; the maxim is that *strong generic structures allow freedoms*. I think it matters very much that, every so often, you sit back and look at your planning and ask yourself where the moments are when children can really develop personal enthusiasms. In the end, as in all aspects of teaching and learning, it must be their momentum, not yours, that carries them through.

Answers

As far as I can tell (never having seen an authoritative list), Craig Raine's Martian (Chapter 4) is describing:

Books
Mist
Rain
A car
A clock and a watch
A telephone
The toilet
Dreams

Also in Chapter 4, U. A. Fanthorpe's vegetables are

Onions
Marrow
Carrots
Leeks
Potatoes
Beetroots

And the final line is

Where we are going

Bibliography

Books about English and teaching

Crystal, D. (1996) *Rediscover Grammar*, Harlow, Longman.

Crystal, D. (1997) *The Cambridge Encyclopedia of the English Language*, Cambridge, Cambridge University Press.

Davies, C. (1996) *What is English Teaching*, Oxford, Oxford University Press.

Davison, J. and Dowson, J. (2003) *Learning to Teach English in the Secondary School*, London, RoutledgeFalmer.

Dean, G. (2003) *Teaching English in the Key Stage 3 Literacy Strategy*, London, Fulton.

Framework for Teaching English: Years 7, 8 and 9, DFES, reference 0019/2001.

Gardner, H. et al. (2003) *Multiple Intelligences: Best Ideas from Theory and Practice*, Harlow, Allyn and Bacon.

Gibson, R. (1998) *Teaching Shakespeare*, Cambridge, Cambridge University Press.

Books about drama

Brandes, D. (1982) *Gamesters' Handbook Two*, Cheltenham, Stanley Thornes.

Brandes, D. and Phillips, H. (1977) *Gamesters' Handbook*, Cheltenham, Stanley Thornes.

Johnstone, K. (1981) *Impro*, London, Methuen.

Rawlins, G. and Rich, J. (1985) *Look, Listen and Trust*, Basingstoke, Macmillan.

Scher, A. and Verall, C. (1975) *100+ Ideas for Drama*, Oxford, Heinemann.

Theodorou, M. (1989) *Ideas that work in Drama*, Cheltenham, Stanley Thornes.

Texts

Chapter 1

Shakespeare texts are available from many publishers and, copyright-free, on the world wide web. The Cambridge school editions are the best teaching editions.

Chapter 2

Almond, D. (1998) *Skellig*, London, Hodder.
Causley, C. *Timothy Winters* (poem) is available in various anthologies.

Chapter 4

Fanthorpe, U. A. (1978) *Side Effects*, Calstock, Peterloo Poets.
—— (2005) *Collected Poems 1978–2003*, Calstock, Peterloo Poets.
Raine, C. (1979) *A Martian Sends a Postcard Home*, Oxford, Oxford University Press.

Chapter 8

Atwood, M. (1996) *The Handmaid's Tale*, New York, Vintage.
Lee, H. (1966) *To Kill a Mockingbird*, Oxford, Heinemann Windmill.
Miller, A. (1994) *Death of a Salesman*, Oxford, Heinemann.
Orwell, G. (1994) *Animal Farm*, London, Penguin.
Priestley, J. B. (1993) *An Inspector Calls*, Oxford, Heinemann.
Steinbeck, J. (1965) *Of Mice and Men*, Oxford, Heinemann Windmill.
Wertenbaker, T. (1995) *Our Country's Good*, London, Methuen.

Index

throughline 65, 67, 96
Timothy Winters see Causley, C.
To Kill a Mocking Bird see Lee, H.
transition points 37
transitions 10, 15, 65–7
trial activity 128
triangulate 40, 166
TTA *see* text-type analysis
Twelfth Night see Shakespeare

valuing and validating pupil
    responses 71–2
variety, planning for 24–6
vertical approach *see* starter
video 4
visual symbol 137

warm up 10, 15, 144
Wertenbaker, T. *Our Country's
    Good* 119
whiteboard 72
whole-body yawns 144
word association and word
    disassociation *see* Games
Wordsworth, W. *London* 51
Working with big texts 111–130
workshop133
writer's intention 48
Wuthering Heights see Bronte, E.

YAVA (You Ask, Volunteers
    Answer) 72–3, 83, 160
Yes, and *see* Games